knit tricks!

Easy Shaping Techniques

25 Stylish Projects from Simple Rectangles

Rebecca Wat

C&T PUBLISHING

Text copyright © 2007 by Rebecca Wat

Artwork copyright © 2007 by C&T Publishing, Inc.

Publisher: Amy Marson

Editorial Director: Gailen Runge

Acquisitions Editor: Jan Grigsby

Editors: Kathleen Greco, Nick Greco, and Kesel Wilson

Technical Editors: Wendy Rogers and Sue Astroth

Copyeditor/Proofreader: Wordfirm, Inc.

Design Director/Cover & Book Designer: Christina D. Jarumay

Production Coordinator: Matt Allen

Illustrators: Deborah Davis and Tim Manibusan

Photography by Luke Mulks and Diane Pedersen of C&T
Publishing, Inc., unless otherwise noted

Published by C&T Publishing, Inc., P.O. Box 1456,
Lafayette, CA 94549

Library of Congress Cataloging-in-Publication Data

Wat, Rebecca,

  Knit tricks! : 25 stylish projects from simple rectangles /
Rebecca Wat.

    p. cm.

  ISBN-13: 978-1-57120-459-2 (paperback : paper trade : alk. paper)

  ISBN-13: 978-1-57120-535-3 (hardcover : alk. paper)

  1. Knitting--Patterns. I. Title.

  TT820.W284 2007

  746.43'2041--dc22

                  2007015323

Printed in China

10 9 8 7 6 5 4 3 2 1

contents

INTRODUCTION

Tired of knitting the same scarf time after time with no end in sight? How about always knitting garments from the bottom up? Do you always knit sweaters by combining separate sections? Why not try making it all in one piece? How about working them from the top down, sideways, sleeve first, center first, or even border first? The purpose of this book is to explore the limitless possibilities of knitting smart, attractive garments using a simple rectangular form with little or no shaping. It's always fun and exciting to explore making garments differently and more efficiently. Many of the 25 projects presented in *Knit Tricks!* utilize non-conventional knitting methods that will take your knitting to a higher dimension. As people always say, "The possibilities are endless."

GETTING STARTED

This book is organized by apparel type, with each project accompanied by a schematic. Skill levels are listed for each project. *Beginner* projects use basic knit and purl stitches with little or no shaping. *Easy* projects use basic stitches, repetitive stitch patterns, simple color changes, and basic shaping and finishing. *Advanced beginner* projects use a variety of stitches including basic cables, lace, double-pointed needles, knitting in the round techniques, and mid-level shaping and finishing.

Before you begin a project, it's important to choose the right size and to match the specified gauge. Instead of wrapping a measuring tape around your body, it is easier to determine the size by measuring an existing garment that fits you comfortably. If the measurement falls between sizes, choose the larger size. You may need to switch needle sizes to match the gauge—if so, ignore the recommended sizes in the pattern. Again, take the time to determine the proper size and knit a four-inch square to check your gauge. The correct gauge will guarantee a comfortable fit.

Keep in mind that the specific yarns listed with each pattern are only suggested yarns. You can certainly substitute different yarns of the *same weight and gauge*, according to your own personal preference.

When you first encounter a complicated stitch pattern or knitting technique, you should test it on a small sample. In addition, don't be afraid to correct any mistakes by unraveling the stitches and starting over. It's more rewarding to have desirable results, even if it means taking more time!

If you're a new knitter or just need a refresher, you'll find all of the required knitting techniques for each project in *Knitting Basics* (page 82). In addition, I have included a list of common knitting *Abbreviations* and their meanings (page 93) to help get you started. Have fun!

ponchos

PONCHOS ARE FASHIONABLE IN ALL SHAPES, LENGTHS, and styles. There are circular ponchos knit from the bottom up with shaping around the shoulders and neck, rectangular ones with center openings, triangular ones made by connecting rectangles, and cylindrical ones knit in ribs. This chapter features ponchos knit from a single rectangle!

Four ponchos are presented: Cardigan and Oriental Ponchos, which are knit right to left, and Ruffled and Cable Border Ponchos, which are knit from the bottom up. They're all designed with simple Stockinette, Single Ribbing, and Cable stitch patterns, with little or no shaping. Simplicity, combined with such stylish details as ruffles and contrasting-color borders, which add interest and glamour, makes them great fun to knit!

cardigan poncho

THE CARDIGAN PONCHO is knit very much like a scarf. The only difference is that the buttons are strategically located along the edge of the "scarf" so that it resembles a cardigan when worn. This poncho is worked right to left in one continuous piece. Ruffles for the right front with three buttonholes are made first. The back, left front, and left-front ruffles complete the poncho. The ruffles are easily created by switching to larger needles, rather than changing the number of stitches.

cardigan poncho

SKILL LEVEL

Beginner

SIZE

One size fits most

FINISHED MEASUREMENTS

- 44″ (112cm) wide × 26″ (66cm) long

YARN

- 3 balls Anny Blatt *Fine Kid* 280yds (258m) / 50g (51% pure wool, 49% kid mohair) Color: 632

YARDAGE

- 840yds (775m)

NEEDLES

- One pair size US 6 (4mm) and US 11 (8mm) needles, or size to obtain gauge

GAUGE

- 18 sts and 25 rows = 4″ (10cm) over Stockinette stitch patt using size US 11 (8mm) needles

- 12 sts and 15 rows = 4″ (10cm) over Stockinette stitch patt using size US 6 (4mm) needles

FINISHING MATERIALS

- 3 buttons ⅝″ (1.5cm)

STOCKINETTE STITCH PATTERN

- Row 1: Knit across.

- Row 2: Purl across.

- Repeat Rows 1 and 2.

cardigan poncho pattern

FRONT OR BACK (ONE PIECE)

- With US 11 needles, CO 120 sts.

- Work in St st for 10″ (25cm), ending with the (WS) facing.

- Change to US 6 needles.

- Work 2 rows in St st.

Buttonholes

- Row 1: K3, BO 2 sts tightly, K to the end.

- Row 2: P to the last 3 sts, CO 2 sts tightly, P3.

- Work 12 rows in St st patt.

- Repeat the above 14 rows once.

- Repeat Rows 1 and 2 (for a total of 3 buttonholes).

- Continue working in St st until work measures 44″ (112cm).

- Change to US 11 needles and work 10″ (25cm) in St st.

- BO all sts.

FINISHING

With (WS) facing, turn in 5″ (12.75cm) at both ends of the piece. Secure with pins and stitch in place. Attach buttons.

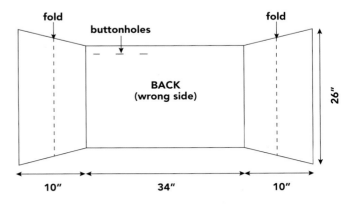

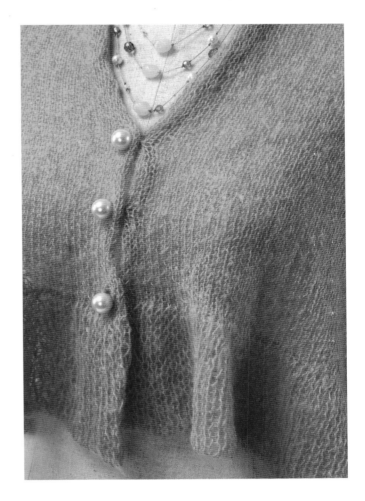

oriental poncho

THE ORIENTAL PONCHO is made from a single rectangle and is knit exactly like a scarf. It is worked from one side to the other (it doesn't matter whether you start from the left or the right). The Spine stitch pattern produces a rather stiff texture for the Ching dynasty style collar. The contrasting border and the three-loop frog buttons will enhance the collar and add elegance to the piece.

SKILL LEVEL

Easy

SIZE

One size fits most

FINISHED MEASUREMENTS

- 44″ (112 cm) wide × 20″ (51cm) long

YARN

- 8 balls Rowan *Kid Classic* 151yds (140m) / 50g (70% lamb's wool, 26% kid mohair, 4% nylon) Color: 825 (A)

- 1 ball Filatura di Crosa *Batuffolo Print* 66yds (61m) / 50g (35% polyamide, 30% wool, 20% acrylic, 15% alpaca) Color: 6 (B)

YARDAGE

- Rowan: 1100yds (1015m)
- Filatura di Crosa: 40yds (37m)

NEEDLES

- One pair size US 11 (8mm) needles, or size to obtain gauge
- Cable needle

CROCHET HOOK

- One size US I-9 (5.5mm) hook

GAUGE

- 15 sts and 14 rows = 4″ (10cm) with 2 strands of A held tog over Spine stitch patt using size US 11 (8mm) needles

FINISHING MATERIALS

- 3 frogs 5″ (12.75cm) × 2″ (5cm)

SPINE STITCH PATTERN

- Row 1: (RS) *Tw2R, Tw2L*, rep from * to * to the end.
- Row 2: (WS) P all sts.

- **Tw2R:** Sl 1 st to cable needle and hold in back of work. K1, then knit the st from the cable needle.

- **Tw2L:** Sl 1 st to the cable needle and hold in front of work. K1, then knit the st from the cable needle.

oriental poncho pattern

BACK

- With US 11 needles and 2 strands A held tog, CO 76 sts.

- Row 1: K across.

- Row 2: P across.

- Row 3: *Tw2R, Tw2L*, rep from * to * to the end.

- Row 4: P across.

- Repeat Rows 3 and 4 until work measures 44˝ (112cm).

- BO all sts.

BORDER

With crochet hook and B, work 1 row in single crochet (page 89) around all edges.

Alternatively, you could crochet a chain (page 88) the same length as the perimeter of the poncho and sew it along the edges. A second border of fur yarn can be sewn on as a single or double strand.

FINISHING

For frog buttons, (RS) back facing, measure in from the left and top edges for placement and attach: 1st frog button: 10˝ from left edge, 2˝ from top edge. 2nd frog button: 8½˝ from left edge, 5˝ from top edge. 3rd frog button: 5˝ from left edge, 7˝ from top edge. Tack frog button loops (along edge) and frog buttons and adjust for fit, before sewing in place.

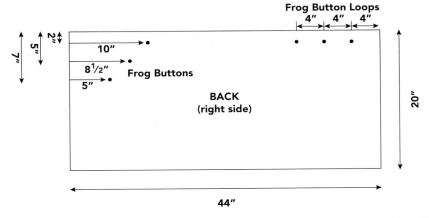

ruffled poncho

THE RUFFLED PONCHO is knit like a rectangle, shaped by simply changing from larger to smaller needles to create a smooth, uninterrupted ribbing pattern. Construct this poncho from the bottom up, starting with the bottom ruffle followed by the two borders in the same yarn. The body is worked next with a different yarn. Finally, the borders and body are joined, and the top ruffle is knit with the border yarn. The poncho can be worn with buttons or a brooch. Try wearing it high around the neck or low around the shoulders.

SKILL LEVEL

Easy

SIZE

One size fits most

FINISHED MEASUREMENTS

- 50″ (127cm) wide × 16″ (40.5cm) long

YARN

- 3 balls Cascade *Pastaza* 132yds (122m) / 100g (50% llama, 50% wool) Color: 064 (A)
- 1 ball Tahki Stacy Charles *Donegal Tweed* 183yds (169m) / 100g (100% pure new wool) Color: 895 (B)

YARDAGE

- Cascade: 396yds (340m)
- Tahki Stacy Charles: 183yds (169m)

NEEDLES

- One pair size US 6 (4mm), US 8 (5mm), US 10 (6mm), and US 11 (8mm) circular needles, or size to obtain gauge

GAUGE

- 14 sts and 21 rows = 4″ (10cm) over Single Rib patt using size US 10 (6mm) needles with A

FINISHING MATERIALS

- 9 buttons ¾″ (1.25cm)

STOCKINETTE STITCH PATTERN

- Row 1: K across.
- Row 2: P across.
- Repeat Rows 1 and 2.

SINGLE RIBBING PATTERN

- Row 1: *P1, K1.
- Repeat from * to end of row.

ruffled poncho pattern

FRONT OR BACK

Bottom Ruffle

- With US 11 needles and B, CO 400 sts.

- Work 6 rows in St st patt.

Right Border (with buttonholes)

- With (RS) facing, change to US 8 needles and work the first 6 sts as follows:

- Row 1: Sl 1, P1, K2tog, YO, K1, P1.

- Row 2: Sl 1, (P1, K1) twice, P1.

- Working in Single Rib, rep Row 2, 10 more times.

- Repeat the above 12 rows 7 more times (8 buttonholes).

- Repeat Rows 1 and 2 once (9 buttonholes).

- Slip these 6 sts onto a holder or safety pin.

Left Border

- With (RS) facing, attach yarn and work the last 6 sts in Single Rib patt until length matches the right border.

- Slip these 6 sts onto a holder or safety pin.

Body

- Decrease row: With (RS) facing, change to US 10 needles and A, *K2tog, P2tog*, rep from * to * to the end. 194 sts.

- Work in Single Rib st for 7″ (18cm).

- Change to US 8 needles and work 2″ (5cm) in Single Rib patt.

- Change to US 6 needles and work in Single Rib patt until body length matches borders.

Top Border

- With (RS) facing, change to US 11 needles and B. Transfer the 6 sts for the right border to the needle and knit them, knit the 194 sts for the body, transfer the 6 sts for the left border to the needle and knit them. 206 sts.

- Work 4 rows in St st patt.

- BO all sts loosely.

FINISHING

Sew borders to the body. Attach buttons.

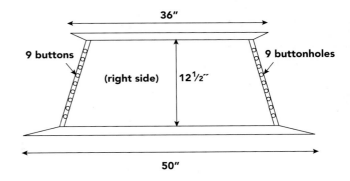

cable border poncho

THE CABLE BORDER PONCHO is knit primarily with the common method for poncho construction—from bottom to top with gradual shaping around the shoulders and neck. What defines the style for this garment is the cable border, which is knit separately. This design is unique because the left and right front borders cross each other twice, creating a cable-in-cable effect. A basic cable pattern for the border was chosen so that beginners can knit it easily. Practice different cable patterns to determine the best cable-in-cable design for you.

cable border poncho

SKILL LEVEL

Advanced Beginner

SIZE

One size fits most

FINISHED MEASUREMENTS

- 50″ (127cm) circumference × 19″ (48cm) long

YARN

- 3 balls Noro *Silk Garden* 110yds (100m) / 50g (45% silk, 45% kid mohair, 10% lamb's wool) Color: 239 (A)

- 2 balls Cascade *Pastaza* 132yds (122m) / 100g (50% llama, 50% wool) Color: 085 (B)

YARDAGE

- Noro: 330yds (304m)

- Cascade: 200yds (185m)

NEEDLES

- One pair size US 9 (5.5mm) needles, or size to obtain gauge

- Cable needle

GAUGE

- 16 sts and 20 rows = 4″ (10cm) over Stockinette stitch patt using size US 9 (5.5mm) needles and A

STOCKINETTE STITCH PATTERN

- Row 1: K across.

- Row 2: P across.

- Repeat Rows 1 and 2.

cable border poncho pattern

BACK (ONE PIECE)

- With US 9 needles and A, CO 200 sts.

- Work St st patt for 10″ (25cm), end with (WS).

- Next row: *K4, K2tog*, rep from * to * to last 2 sts, K2. 167 sts.

- Work 7 rows in St st patt.

- Next row: *K4, K2tog*, rep from * to * to last 5 sts, K5. 140 sts.

- Work 7 rows in St st patt.

- Next row: *K4, K2tog*, rep from * to * to last 2 sts, K2. 117 sts.

- Work 7 rows in St st patt.

- Next row: *K4, K2tog*, rep from * to * to last 3 sts, K3. 98 sts.

- Work 7 rows in St st patt.

- Next row: *K4, K2tog*, repeat from * to * to last 2 sts, K2. 82 sts.

- Work 7 rows in St st patt.

- BO all sts.

CABLE BORDER

- With US 9 needles and B, CO 12 sts.

- Row 1: (RS) P2, K8, P2.

- Row 2: (WS) K2, P8, K2.

- Repeat Rows 1 and 2 once.

Work Cable pattern as follows:

- Row 1: P2, slip 4 sts to cable needle, place in front, K4 from left needle, K4 from cable needle, P2.

- Rows 2, 4, 6, 8, and 10: K2, P8, K2.

- Rows 3, 5, 7, and 9: P2, K8, P2.

- Repeat above 10 rows until work matches length of the perimeter of the body, approx 125″ (3.2m).

- BO all sts.

FINISHING

Arrange side cable edges tog crossing in front. Baste border along edges. Stitch in place.

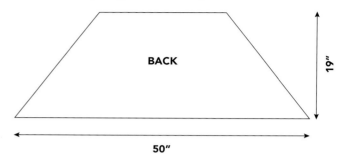

BACK

19″

50″

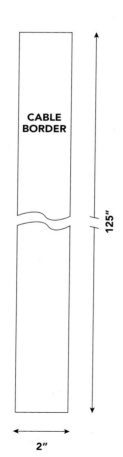

CABLE BORDER

125″

2″

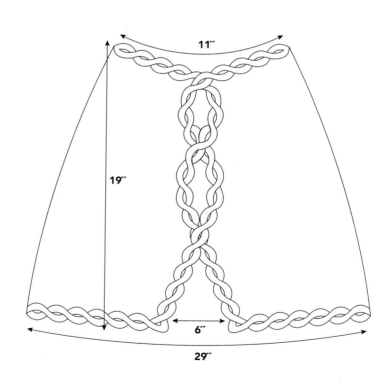

11″

19″

6″

29″

shrugs

SHRUGS ARE SO FEMININE! THESE STYLISH KNITS are loose fitting, comfortable, and fun to wear. What may surprise you is how easy they are to make. Simple rectangles are knit from either the side or the bottom.

The Denim Jacket and Ruffled Shrugs are knit from one rectangle, while the unique Scarf Shrug takes two. Simple Garter, Stockinette, and Single Ribbing stitches are used; just change the needle size for super, trouble-free shaping. Collars, cuffs, lace, and ruffles are made separately and attached during assembly for a dazzling, decorative finish. Essential for every wardrobe, these fashion-savvy shrugs are one-size-fits-most.

denim jacket shrug

DENIM JACKETS ARE VERSATILE, DURABLE, AND TIMELESS. The inspiration for this knit version comes from a denim jacket with a fleece lining. To make this shrug, begin knitting a large rectangle from the bottom up in a Single Ribbing pattern. Next, add the collar and cuffs, and sew the sides together to complete the sleeves. The Single Ribbing stitch provides plenty of elasticity and makes this pattern work for all sizes. To adjust the arm measurements, simply lengthen or shorten the cuffs!

denim jacket shrug

SKILL LEVEL

Beginner

SIZE

One size fits most

FINISHED MEASUREMENTS

- 58″ (147cm) from cuff to cuff × 16″ (41cm) long (Note: Because the single rib stretches and (B) yarn is bulky, the garment measurement cuff-to-cuff can vary.)

YARN

- 5 balls Di.Ve' *Teseo Yarns* 98yds (90m) / 50g (55% wool, 45% microfiber) Color: 47188 (A)

- 5 balls Austermann *Bouclerone* 16.5yds (15m) / 50g (60% virgin wool, 34% acrylic, 6% polyester) Color: 101 (B)

YARDAGE

- Di.Ve': 490yds (452m)

- Austermann: 74yds (68m)

NEEDLES

- One pair size US 10 (6mm) and US 15 (10mm) circular needles, or size to obtain gauge

GAUGE

- 12 sts and 16 rows = 4″ (10cm) with A over Single Rib stitch patt using US 10 (6mm) needles

- 6 sts and 9 rows = 4″ (10m) with B over Garter stitch patt using US 15 (10mm) needles

SINGLE RIBBING PATTERN

- Row 1: *P1, K1.

- Repeat from * to end of row.

GARTER STITCH PATTERN

- K every row.

denim jacket shrug pattern

BODY AND SLEEVES

- With US 10 needles and A, CO 150 sts.

- Work in Single Rib patt until piece measures 16″ (40.5cm).

- BO all sts.

COLLAR AND BORDER (MAKE 2)

- With (RS) facing, US 10 needles, and B, pick up 60 sts evenly across the center 60 sts of the bind-off edge.

- Change to US 15 needles and work loosely in Garter st patt for 3″ (7.5cm).

- BO all sts.

- Repeat on cast-on edge of body.

CUFFS (MAKE 2)

- With (RS) facing, US 10 needles, and B, pick up 34 sts evenly along the edge of one sleeve.

- Work loosely in Garter st patt for 2½″ (6.5cm).

- BO off sts.

- Repeat for other sleeve.

FINISHING

Fold in half and sew the underarm seams tog. Join collar/border edges to make a continuous loop. Join cuff edges.

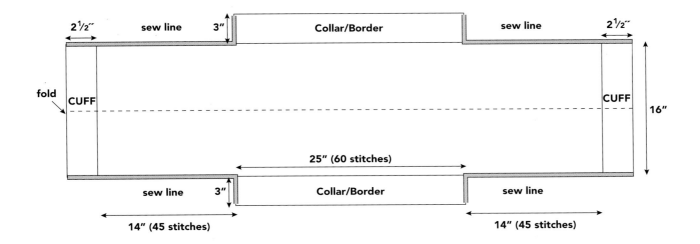

ruffled shrug

RUFFLES ARE FUN to make and add elegance and interest to this lightweight but warm mohair Ruffled Shrug. Like the Denim Jacket Shrug, this delicate garment is made from a large rectangle, which forms the body and sleeves. Ruffles are added to create the collar and cuffs. This pattern is designed without intricate shaping—just right for beginner knitters. Just change needle size and work in a Stockinette stitch pattern. To adjust arm length, simply lengthen or shorten the cuffs.

SKILL LEVEL

Beginner

SIZE

One size fits most

FINISHED MEASUREMENTS

- 55″ (140cm) from cuff to cuff × 26″ long

YARN

- 4 balls Galler Yarns *Flore II* 100yds (91m) / 50g (75% kid mohair, 15% wool, 10% nylon) Color: 014 (A)

- 2 balls Bouton d'Or *Arpege* 126yds (115m) / 50g (78% kid mohair, 22% wool) Color: 231 (B)

YARDAGE

- Galler Yarns: 400yds (369m)

- Bouton d'Or: 252yds (231m)

NEEDLES

- One pair size US 15 (10mm) and US 6 (4mm) circular needles, or size to obtain gauge

GAUGE

- 11 sts and 12 rows = 4″ (10cm) over Stockinette stitch patt using US 15 (10mm) needles with A or B

- 18 sts and 20 rows = 4″ (10cm) over Stockinette stitch patt using US 6 (4mm) needles with A

STOCKINETTE STITCH PATTERN

- Row 1: K across.

- Row 2: P across.

- Repeat Rows 1 and 2.

ruffled shrug pattern

BODY AND SLEEVES

- With US 6 needles and A, CO 70 sts.

- Work 5 rows in St st patt.

- Change to US 15 needles and cont in St st patt until work measures 48″ (122cm).

- Change to US 6 needles and work 5 rows in St st patt.

- BO all sts.

SLEEVE RUFFLES

- With (RS) facing, US 6 needles, and B, pick up 70 sts along one side edge. Change to US 15 needles and work in St st patt for 2″ (5cm), ending with the (WS).

- Increase row: Inc 1 st on every other st. 105 sts.

- P1 row.

- BO all sts loosely.

- Repeat for other side.

- Fold piece in half and sew ruffle edges tog. Sew 10″ (25cm) sleeve seams (leave center open).

COLLAR RUFFLES

- Mark 8½″ (21.5cm) in from either end of the opening for the collar.

- With (RS) facing, US 6 needles, and B, pick up 138 sts evenly (3 sts per inch) around the marked length.

- Change to US 15 needles and work in St st patt for 2″ (5cm), ending with the (WS).

- Increase row: Inc 1 st on every other st. 207 sts.

- P1 row.

- BO all sts loosely.

FINISHING

Sew the side edges of the collar ruffles in place.

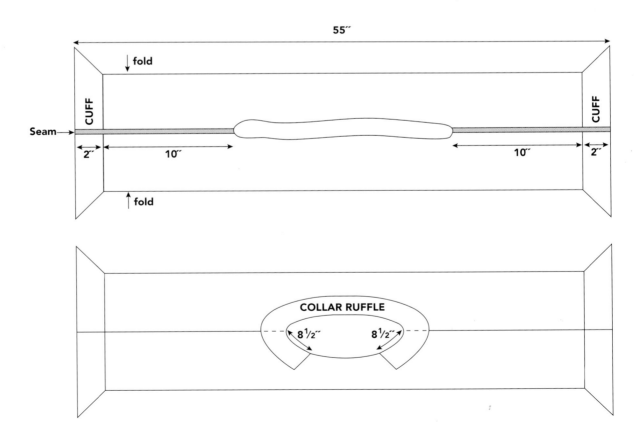

scarf shrug

IT'S A SHRUG WITH A SCARF—both stylish and practical!
The beautiful blend of mohair, wool, and silk gives this shrug a
luxurious feel. The sleeves, knit out of two rectangles, are made
first. The scarf, front, and back are extensions of the sleeves. The
lace edging may be a little challenging for beginning knitters,
but it is knit separately. The Scarf Shrug can be made without
the lace trim and still look very fashionable.

scarf shrug

SKILL LEVEL

Advanced Beginner

SIZE

One size fits most

FINISHED MEASUREMENTS

- 60″ (152cm) from cuff to cuff × 14″ (35.5cm) long

YARN

- 9 balls Artfibers *Kyoto* 110yds (100m) / 50g (69% silk, 25% kid mohair, 6% wool) Color: 30

YARDAGE

- 990yds (914m)

NEEDLES

- One pair size US 10 (6mm) circular needles, or size to obtain gauge

GAUGE

- 14 sts and 17 rows = 4″ (10cm) over Stockinette stitch patt using size US 10 (6mm) circular needles

STOCKINETTE STITCH PATTERN

- Row 1: K across.
- Row 2: P across.
- Repeat Rows 1 and 2.

scarf shrug pattern

RIGHT SLEEVE

- With US 10 needles, CO 84 sts.
- Work in St st for 24″ (61cm), ending with (WS).
- Separate row: K42 sts, slip next 42 sts onto a stitch holder.
- Work the remaining 42 sts in St st for another 30″ (76cm) for the scarf.
- BO these 42 sts.
- Pick up the 42 sts from the stitch holder and work in St st for 12″ (30.5cm) for the back.
- BO all sts.

LEFT SLEEVE

- With US 10 needles, CO 84 sts.
- Work in St st for 24″ (61cm), ending with (WS).
- K42 sts, BO next 42 sts.

- Rejoin yarn and cont in St st on the remaining 42 sts for 10″ (25cm) for the left front.
- BO all sts.

LACE EDGING

- With US 10 needles, CO 4 sts.
- K1 row across.

The following 8 rows form the pattern:

- Increase Rows 1, 3, 5, and 7: K to last 2 sts, YO, K2.
- Rows 2, 4, and 6: Sl 1 knitwise, K to end.
- Row 8: BO 4 sts, K to end.
- Repeat these 8 rows until the border length matches the total length of the edges of the work.

FINISHING

Sew the back seam (see Horizontal Invisible Seam, page 92) and then the underarm seams. Baste and stitch the lace border along the scarf, back, and front edges of the garment.

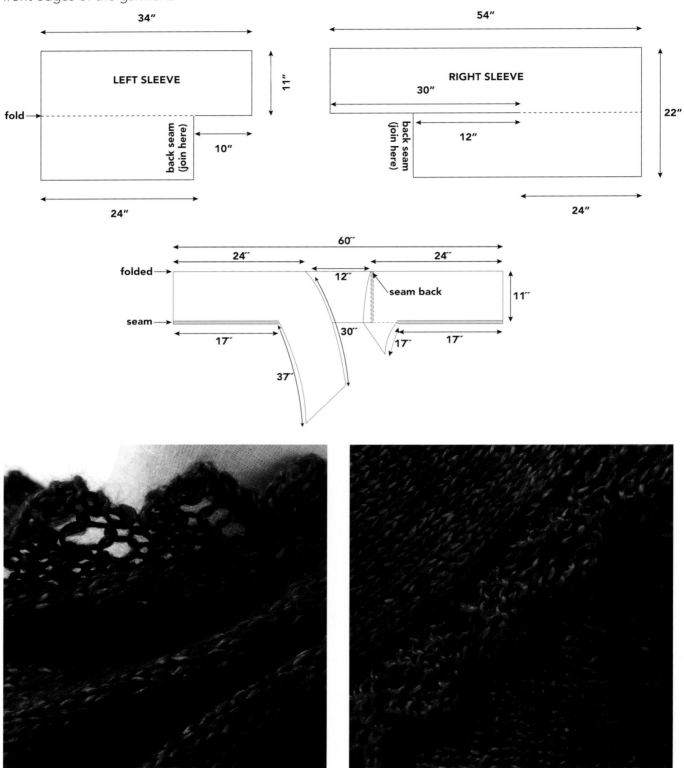

tops

RECTANGULAR SCARVES AND SLEEVELESS TOPS ARE EASY
projects to knit. Create sleeveless, drop-shoulder tops simply by
sewing two knitted rectangles together, leaving openings for your
head and arms. These seven cleverly designed projects feature a
variety of necklines and waistlines, with no shaping.

Accent the Empress Waist Top and Bow-in-Collar Top with woven
ribbons. Embellish the neckline of your tops by incorporating a
necklace with the Embedded Necklace Top, create a draped collar in
the Turn-out-Collar Top, or knit a cable neckline border from the top
down in the Cable Collar Top. Fashion two beautiful tops by knitting
two rectangles in the Tie Shoulder Top or make two long scarves to
complete the Big Cross Top. Enjoy creating these simple designs and
marvel at the dramatic results. In fact, that's the idea behind the
designs in this chapter—they're simply marvelous!

empress waist top

OCCASIONALLY, SOMETHING AS SIMPLE as a piece of ribbon is all you need to create or complete a style. This delicate Empress Waist Top is knit in two simple rectangles with soft mohair yarn in Stockinette stitch pattern. Accentuate the empire waistline with a velvet ribbon slipped through a yarn over lace row. For quick-and-easy finishing, sew side seams and tie a perfect bow in the middle—just the right touch for this classic style.

empress waist top

SKILL LEVEL

Beginner

SIZE

XS (S, M, L, XL)

FINISHED MEASUREMENTS

- Chest 34 (36, 38, 40, 42)″ / 86 (91.5, 96.5, 102, 107)cm
- Length 21″ (53cm)

YARN

- 6 (7, 7, 7, 8) balls Lion Brand Yarns *Moonlight Mohair* 82yds (75m) / 50g (57% acrylic, 28% mohair, 9% cotton, 6% polyester metallic) Color: 202

YARDAGE

- 480 (510, 540, 570, 600)yds / 443 (471, 498, 526, 554)m

NEEDLES

- One pair size US 11 (8mm) needles, or size to obtain gauge

GAUGE

- 11.5 sts and 12 rows = 4″ (10cm) over Stockinette stitch patt using size US 11 (8mm) needles

FINISHING MATERIALS

- 2 yds (1.8m) Velvet ribbon 1″ (2.5cm) wide

GARTER STITCH PATTERN

- K every row.

STOCKINETTE STITCH PATTERN

- Row 1: K across.
- Row 2: P across.
- Repeat Rows 1 and 2.

empress waist top pattern

BACK AND FRONT (MAKE 2)

- With US 11 needles, CO 50 (52, 56, 58, 62) sts.

- Work 6 rows in Garter st patt, ending with (WS).

- Beginning with a K row, cont in St st patt until work measures 9″ (23cm), ending with (WS).

Lace Row

- Next row: (RS) P across.

- Next row: (WS) K across.

- Next row: (RS) K2, *K2tog, YO*, repeat from * to * to last 2 sts, K2.

- Next row: K across.

- Next row: P across.

Continue Back and Front

- Cont in St st until work measures 21″ (53cm).

- BO all sts.

FINISHING

Sew shoulder seams tog 4″ (10cm) on each side.
Sew side seams tog 12″ (30.5cm) from bottom edge.

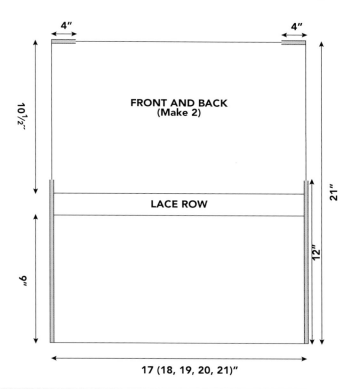

embedded necklace top

DO YOU LIKE NECKLACES? Well, this one comes with a special top. The Embedded Necklace Top is knit sideways in two identical rectangles in a stylish vertical ribbing texture. String large crystal beads through the top edge, shaping the neck. The beaded drawstring creates a ruffled-edged neckline without knitting. The number of cast-on stitches determines the length, and the rows determine the width. Have fun matching different beads with different yarn colors. It's fun and fashionable!

embedded necklace top

SKILL LEVEL

Beginner

SIZES

XS (S, M, L, XL)

FINISHED MEASUREMENTS

- Chest 34 (36, 38, 40, 42)″ / 86 (91.5, 96.5, 102, 107)cm

- Length 21″ (53cm)

YARN

- 5 (6, 6, 7, 7) balls Artfibers *Basque* 110yds (100m) / 50g (58% silk, 42% super kid mohair) Color: 9

YARDAGE

- 550 (592, 630, 676, 718)yds / 507 (546, 581, 624, 662)m

NEEDLES

- One pair size US 9 (5.5mm) needles, or size to obtain gauge

GAUGE

- 15 sts and 32 rows = 4″ (10cm) over Garter stitch patt using size US 9 (5.5mm) needles

FINISHING MATERIALS

- 20 crystal beads size ⅝″ (1.5cm)

GARTER STITCH PATTERN

- K every row.

embedded necklace top pattern

BACK AND FRONT (MAKE 2)

- With US 9 needles, CO 80 sts.

- Row 1: K across.

- Rows 2–9: K across.

- Row 10: P across.

- Row 11: K across.

- Row 12: P across.

- Row 13: K across.

- Repeat Rows 2–13 until work measures 17 (18, 19, 20, 21)″ / 43 (45.5, 48, 51, 53)cm.

- BO all sts.

FINISHING

Sew side seams tog 10″ (25cm) from the bottom and 1.5″ (3.75cm) from the top edge, leaving a 9.5″ (24cm) armhole. Sew beads, either individually or in a chain, along the neckline. Secure beads by running the thread through the hole in the bead a few times, catching the fabric in the back.

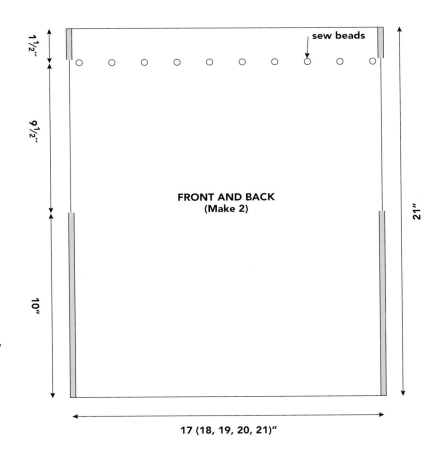

sew beads

1½″

9½″

10″

FRONT AND BACK
(Make 2)

21″

17 (18, 19, 20, 21)″

cable collar top

HAVE YOU EVER STARTED KNITTING A sweater from the collar down? Begin constructing the Cable Collar Top by knitting a cable-edged band for the collar. Pick up stitches along the collar, and then knit front and back pieces individually. The piece is worked in a soft, thick wool blend, using Stockinette stitch, and is finished with a ribbed waistband. Knitters who prefer knitting in the round can start beneath the armhole. This project offers an easy way to knit and assemble a sweater top with cables.

SKILL LEVEL

Advanced Beginner

SIZES

XS (S, M, L, XL)

FINISHED MEASUREMENTS

Chest 34 (36, 38, 40, 42)″ /
86 (91.5, 96.5, 102, 107)cm

Length 19″ (48cm)

YARN

6 (6, 7, 7, 7) balls Rowan
Little Big Wool 66yds (61m)
/ 50g (67% wool, 33% nylon)
Color: 501

YARDAGE

342 (372, 402, 432, 462)yds /
315 (343, 371, 399, 426)m

NEEDLES

One pair size US 13 (9mm) and
US 11 (8mm) needles, or size to
obtain gauge

Cable needle

GAUGE

11 sts and 15 rows = 4″ (10cm)
over Stockinette stitch patt
using size US 13 (9mm) needles

STOCKINETTE STITCH PATTERN

Row 1: K across.

Row 2: P across.

Repeat Rows 1 and 2.

cable collar top pattern

CABLE COLLAR
- With US 13 needles, CO 16 sts.

Cable Pattern (8 rows)
- Row 1: K across.
- Row 2: P across.
- Row 3: K across.
- Row 4: P across.
- Row 5: Sl 4 sts to holder (place at back), K4, K4 from holder, Sl 4 sts to holder (place in front), K4, K4 from holder.
- Row 6: P across.
- Row 7: K across.
- Row 8: P across.
- Repeat Rows 1–8 until work measures 30″ (76cm).

BACK
- With size US 11 needles, pick up 48 (51, 54, 57, 60) sts from the center of the cable collar.
- Change to US 13 needles. Cont in St st patt until work measures 17½″ (44.5cm).
- Change to US 11 needles. Work 1½″ (2.5cm) in Single Ribbing patt.
- BO all sts.

FRONT
- Cross the ends of the cable collar, pick up 48 (51, 54, 57, 60) sts with US 11 needles.
- Change to US 13 needles. Cont in St st patt until work measures 17½″ (44.5cm).
- Change to US 11 needles. Work 1½″ (2.5cm) in Single Ribbing patt.
- BO all sts.

FINISHING
Sew side seams tog 8½″ (21.5cm) from the bottom, leaving an 8″ (20cm) armhole.

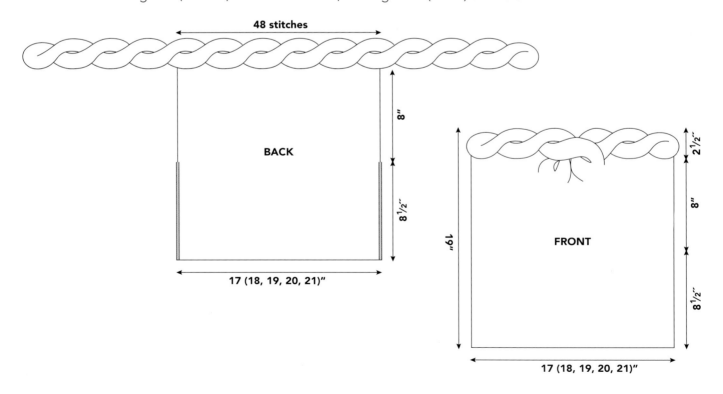

bow-in-collar top

PRETTY RIBBONS can be used in so many ways in knitting. The Bow-in-Collar Top utilizes a wide satin ribbon through the side of the neckline to join the front and back pieces. The ribbon adds to the style as well as the adjustability of this uniquely designed sleeveless sweater. Shaping is created simply by switching from Single Ribbing to Stockinette with different-size needles. As a result, the number of stitches always stays the same. The collar design is created in Single Ribbing.

bow-in-collar top

SKILL LEVEL

Beginner

SIZES

XS (S, M, L, XL)

FINISHED MEASUREMENTS

- Chest 34 (36, 38, 40, 42)″ / 86 (91.5, 96.5, 102, 107)cm
- Length 21″ (53cm)

YARN

- 3 (4, 4, 4, 4) balls Cascade *Pastaza* 132yds (120m) / 100g (50% llama, 50% wool) Color: 75

YARDAGE

- 396 (426, 456, 486, 516)yds / 365 (393, 421, 449, 476)m

NEEDLES

- One pair size US 10.5 (6.5mm) and US 9 (5.5mm) needles, or size to obtain gauge

GAUGE

- 15 sts and 14 rows = 4″ (10cm) over Stockinette stitch patt using size US 10.5 (6.5mm) needles

FINISHING MATERIALS

- 2 yds satin ribbon 1″ (2.5cm) wide

STOCKINETTE STITCH PATTERN

- Row 1: K across.
- Row 2: P across.
- Repeat Rows 1 and 2.

SINGLE RIBBING PATTERN

- Row 1: *P1, K1.
- Repeat from * to end of row.

bow-in-collar top pattern

FRONT AND BACK (MAKE 2)

- With US 9 needles, CO 66 (70, 74, 78, 82) sts.
- Work in Single Ribbing patt for 3″ (7.5cm).
- Change to US 10.5 needles and work in St st until piece measures 17″ (43cm).
- Change to US 9 needles and work in Single Ribbing patt for 4″ (10cm).
- BO all sts.

FINISHING

Sew side seams 9″ (23cm) from the bottom edge. Sew the right side seam 5″ (12.75cm) from the top edge for the right shoulder. Sew 1″ (2.5cm) of the left side seam below the top ribbed area. Lace the ribbon to join the top 4″ (10cm) of the left side seam for the left shoulder. Tie in a bow.

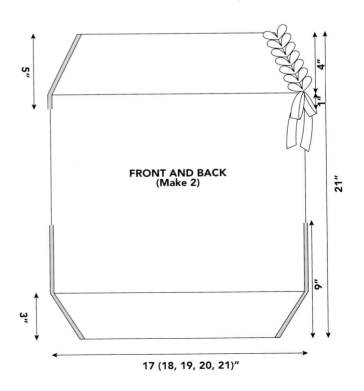

5"

FRONT AND BACK
(Make 2)

21"

9"

3"

4"

1"

17 (18, 19, 20, 21)"

turn-out-collar top

DON'T YOU JUST LOVE DECORATIVE COLLARS? They add style and elegance to your knitwear. The Turn-out-Collar Top is designed with a simple front and back, but adds a beautiful knit-in collar. Create the body as usual, but change yarns with contrasting color and weight. By knitting the collar in a Drop Stitch (page 87) with needles of the same size, the knitted fabric becomes loose while retaining a lovely drape. When you finish knitting, just roll the big collar inside out and watch the magic unfold.

SKILL LEVEL

Easy

SIZES

XS (S, M, L, XL)

FINISHED MEASUREMENTS

- Chest 34 (36, 38, 40, 42)″ / 86 (91.5, 96.5, 102, 107)cm

- Length 20″ (51cm)

YARN

- 5 (5, 6, 6, 6) balls Rowan *All Seasons Cotton* 98yds (90m) / 50g (60% cotton, 40% acrylic) Color: 169 (A)

- 1 ball Noro *Aurora* 114yds (104m) / 40g (55% wool, 20% kid mohair, 20% silk, 5% polyester) Color: 2 (B)

YARDAGE

- Rowan: 460 (490, 520, 550, 580)yds / 424 (452, 480, 508, 535)m

- Noro: 110yds (101m)

NEEDLES

- One pair size US 9 (5.5mm) needles, or size to obtain gauge

GAUGE

- 15 sts and 20 rows = 4″ (10cm) over Stockinette stitch patt using size US 9 (5.5mm) needles with A

GARTER STITCH PATTERN

- K every row.

STOCKINETTE STITCH PATTERN

- Row 1: K across.

- Row 2: P across.

- Repeat Rows 1 and 2.

turn-out-collar top pattern

FRONT

- With US 9 needles and A, CO 64 (68, 72, 76, 80) sts.

- Work 8 rows in Garter st patt.

- Work in St st until piece measures 14″ (35.5cm), ending with (WS).

Shoulder and Collar

- (To switch yarn, loop new yarn around old yarn before knitting.)

- Next row: K10, switch to B, work in Drop st patt to last 10 sts, switch back to A (start a new ball), K10.

- Next row: P10, switch to B, K to last 10 sts, switch back to A, P10.

- Repeat last 2 rows for 6″ (15cm).

- BO all sts (BO Drop sts loosely).

BACK

- With A, CO 64 (68, 72, 76, 80) sts.

- Work 8 rows in Garter stitch patt.

- Cont in St st until work measures 19″ (48cm), ending with (WS).

Neck and Shoulders

- Next row: K10, P to last 10 sts, K10.

- Next row: P across.

- Repeat last 2 rows for 1″ (2.5cm).

- BO all sts.

FINISHING

Sew side seams 10″ from the bottom edge. Sew the shoulder seams. Roll the collar inside out.

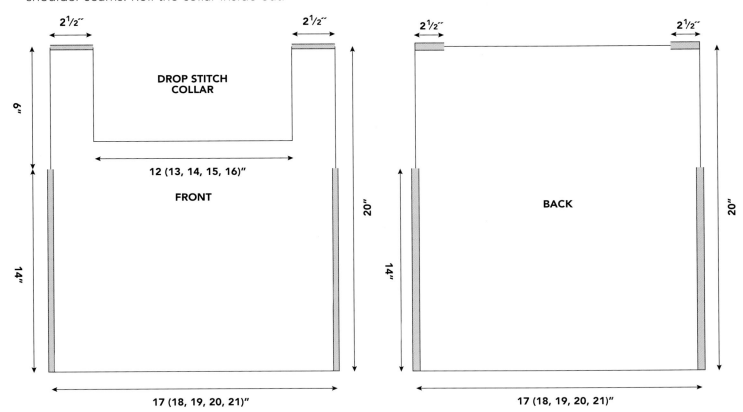

tie shoulder top

THIS UNIQUE TIE SHOULDER TOP TURNS a simple knit construction into an elegant design. Knit two identical rectangles with Shimmer ribbon yarn. Assemble the shoulders by tying the top corners together. Pearl buttons complete the finishing. Picot edges add a delicate embellishment to the top and bottom edges. For a fashionable pillow cover version, tie all the sides together around a pillow form. The elegant styling and simple construction make this top a fashion favorite.

tie shoulder top

SKILL LEVEL

Easy

SIZES

XS (S, M, L, XL)

FINISHED MEASUREMENTS

- Chest 34 (36, 38, 40, 42)″ / 86.5 (91.5, 96.5, 102, 107)cm

- Length 19″ (48cm)

YARN

- 4 (5, 5, 6, 6) balls Crystal Palace *Shimmer* 90yds (82m) / 50g (86% acrylic, 14% nylon) Color: 2849

YARDAGE

- 360 (400, 440, 480, 520)yds / 332 (369, 406, 443, 480)m

NEEDLES

- One pair size US 11 (8mm) needles, or size to obtain gauge

GAUGE

- 15 sts and 19 rows = 4″ (10cm) over Stockinette stitch patt using size US 11 (8mm) needles

FINISHING MATERIALS

- 2 pearl buttons 1″ (2.5cm) wide

STOCKINETTE STITCH PATTERN

- Row 1: K across.

- Row 2: P across.

- Repeat Rows 1 and 2.

tie shoulder top pattern

FRONT AND BACK (MAKE 2)

- With US 11 needles, CO 64 (68, 72, 76, 80) sts.

Picot Edge (the following 4 rows)

- Row 1: K across.

- Row 2: P across.

- Row 3: K1, *K2tog, YO*, repeat from * to * to last st, K1.

- Row 4: P across.

- Work in St st patt until work measures 21″ (53cm), ending with (WS).

Shoulders and Neck with Picot Edge

- Row 1: K8, *K2tog, YO*, repeat from * to * to last 8 sts, K8.

- Work 3 more rows in St st patt.

- BO all sts.

FINISHING

Stitch side seams tog 10″ (25cm) from the bottom for a 9″ (23cm) armhole. For edges along the bottom and neckline, turn under along the picot row and stitch to secure (WS). At shoulder, with wrong sides together, take corner from front and back and tie 2″ from corner point with matching yarn and stitch to secure. Sew on buttons.

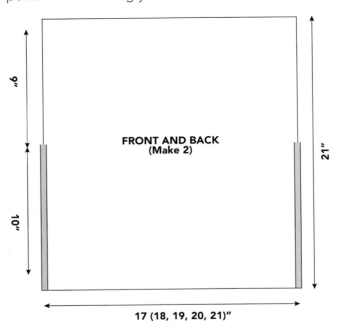

FRONT AND BACK
(Make 2)

9″

10″

21″

17 (18, 19, 20, 21)″

big cross top

TURN TWO SCARVES INTO A SWEATER with this simple, yet versatile, project. Make two long scarves and sew side seams to form two large loops. There are several ways to wear this Big Cross Top. You can wrap the big loops around your waist or let them hang on your shoulders. This garment wears like a sweater, but it's so much more. This top is designed to be reversible, so follow the finishing instructions carefully.

big cross top

SKILL LEVEL

Easy

SIZES

One size fits most

FINISHED MEASUREMENTS

N/A

YARN

- 6 balls Malabrigo *Merino* 216yds (196m) / 3.5oz (100% merino wool) Color: 610 Red Mahogany

YARDAGE

- 1296yds (1196m)

NEEDLES

- One pair size US 9 (5.5mm) needles, or size to obtain gauge

GAUGE

- 18 sts and 23 rows = 4″ (10cm) over Stockinette stitch patt using US 9 (5.5mm) needles

STOCKINETTE STITCH PATTERN

- Row 1: K across.
- Row 2: P across.
- Repeat Rows 1 and 2.

big cross top pattern

SLEEVE AND BODY (MAKE 2)

Sleeve

- With US 9 needles, CO 51 sts.
- Row 1: *P2, K5*, repeat from * to * until last 2 sts, P2.
- Row 2: *K2, P5*, repeat from * to * until last 2 sts, K2.
- Repeat Rows 1 and 2 until work measures 21″ (53cm), ending with (WS).

Body

- Row 1: *P1, K1*, repeat from * to * 3 times,

  P2, K5, repeat from * to * until last 8 sts,

  P1, K1, repeat from * to * 3 times.
- Row 2: *K1, P1*, repeat from * to * 3 times,

  P5, K2, repeat from * to * until last 8 sts,

  K1, P1, repeat from * to * 3 times.

- Repeat last 2 rows for 38″ (96.5cm), ending with (WS). The work measures 59″ (150cm) from beginning to end.

Sleeve

- Repeat sleeve section. Work measures 80″ (230cm).
- BO all sts.

FINISHING

Loop the two scarves around each other (with identical stitch patts facing). Mark and sew the shoulder and arm seams 23″ (58.5cm) for both loops. Mark and sew the underarm seams 19″ (48cm) for both loops.

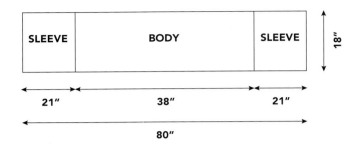

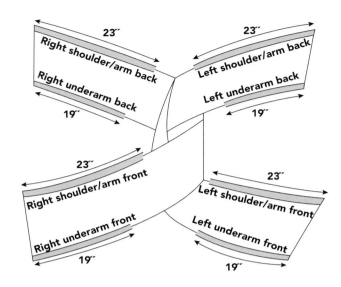

WEARING THE GARMENT

To change styles from wrap-around-waist to wrap-around-shoulders and vice versa, put one sleeve through the loop of the other sleeve.

To wear it on the reverse side, turn both loops inside out.

Whichever way you choose to wear it, for the sleeves to fit, make sure the shoulder seams hang on the shoulders.

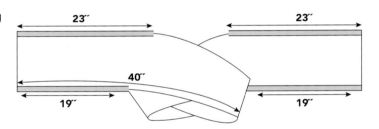

vests

IN TRADITIONAL VEST MAKING, THERE'S A LEFT FRONT, right front, back, long border with buttonholes, and plenty of simultaneous arm, neck, and shoulder shaping. Now there's an easier way. This chapter teaches you how to make vests out of rectangles—no shaping or row counting needed! You'll be knitting rectangles to the required sizes, as in scarf knitting, and then joining them to finish the garment.

With the Big Border Vest, you knit one large rectangle and create a thick border in Garter stitch pattern. The Convertible Vest/Bag is knit from four rectangles and assembled with a separating zipper that allows you to convert easily from a vest to a bag. These projects are less cumbersome and they promise chic, contemporary results.

big border vest

WONDERFUL AND WARM, THE BIG BORDER VEST is a simple yet satisfying project. The large rectangular body is worked in Single Ribbing throughout, with chunky merino wool. Use thick bouclé yarn and large needles to create a big border with a simple Garter stitch pattern. You'll have fun mixing different color yarn combinations to achieve surprising results. Just be sure to match the gauge specified in the pattern. This trouble-free vest is both simple to knit and fun to wear.

big border vest

SKILL LEVEL

Beginner

SIZE

One size fits most

FINISHED MEASUREMENTS

- Chest 36″ (91.5cm) (with ease)
- Length 25″ (63.5cm)

YARN

- 3 balls Malabrigo *Merino* 216yds (196m) / 100g (100% pure merino wool) Color: *Simply Taube* 601 (A)

- 3 balls Filatura di Crosa *Batuffolo Print* 66yds (61m) / 50g (35% polyamide, 30% wool, 20% acrylic, 15% alpaca) Color: 3 (B)

YARDAGE

- Malabrigo: 540yds (498m)
- Filatura di Crosa: 142yds (137m)

NEEDLES

- One pair size US 11 (8mm) and US 15 (10mm) needles, or size to obtain gauge

GAUGE

- 14.5 sts and 16 rows = 4″ (10cm) with A over Single Rib patt using size US 11 (8mm) needles

- 12 sts and 12 rows = 4″ (10cm) with B over Garter stitch patt using size US 15 (10mm) needles

SINGLE RIBBING PATTERN

- Row 1: *K1, P1.
- Repeat from * to end of row.

GARTER STITCH PATTERN

- K every row.

big border vest pattern

FRONT AND BACK

Border
- With US 15 needles and B, CO 85 sts.
- Work in Garter st patt for 5″ (12.75cm).

Body
- Change to US 11 needles and A.
- Row 1: *K1, P1*, repeat from * to * to end.
- Row 2: *P1, K1*, repeat from * to * to end.
- Repeat Rows 1 and 2 until body measures 20″ (50cm).

Border
- Change to US 15 needles and B.
- Work in Garter st patt for 5″ (12.75 cm).
- BO all sts.

FINISHING
Fold piece in half and sew the side seams, leaving the top 6″ (15.25cm) open for armholes.

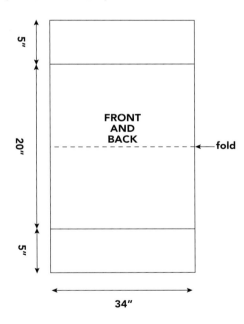

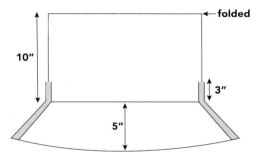

convertible vest/bag

IT'S A VEST THAT CONVERTS TO A BAG! The functional zipper is the inspiration for this one-of-a-kind convertible garment. A two-way separating zipper that opens at both ends makes the conversion possible. The zipper attachment is a useful technique that is easily learned. Experiment with this pattern if you are a little daring and want a garment that is unique in many ways. Wear it as a vest and then convert it to a bag if the weather changes. You'll love the creative versatility of this remarkable garment!

convertible vest/bag

SKILL LEVEL

Advanced Beginner

SIZES

XS (S, M, L, XL)

FINISHED MEASUREMENTS

Chest 34 (36, 38, 40, 42)″ / 86 (91.5, 96.5, 102, 107)cm

Length 21″ (53cm)

YARN

3 (4, 4, 4, 5) balls Cascade *Pastaza* 132yds (118m) / 100g (50% llama, 50% wool) Color: 46 (A)

1 ball Noro *Silk Garden* 110yds (100m) / 50g (45% silk, 45% kid mohair, 10% lamb's wool) Color: 251 (B)

YARDAGE

Cascade: 396 (436, 476, 516, 556)yds / 365 (402, 439, 476, 513)m

Noro: 90yds (83m)

NEEDLES

One pair size US 9 (5.5mm) and US 8 (5mm) needles, or size to obtain gauge

GAUGE

16 sts and 21 rows = 4″ (10cm) with A over Stockinette stitch patt using size US 9 (5.5mm) needles

18 sts and 23 rows = 4″ (10cm) with B over Double Ribbing stitch patt and US 8 (5mm) needles

FINISHING MATERIALS

Separating zipper 31 (32, 33, 34, 35)″ / 79 (81, 84, 86, 89)cm

STOCKINETTE STITCH PATTERN

Row 1: K across.

Row 2: P across.

Repeat Rows 1 and 2.

DOUBLE RIBBING STITCH PATTERN

Row 1: *K2, P2.

Repeat from * to end of row.

convertible vest/bag pattern

LEFT SIDE BACK (WORK FROM BACK TO FRONT)
- With US 9 needles and A, CO 24 (26, 28, 30, 32) sts.
- Work in St st patt for 14″ (35.6cm), ending with (WS).

Armhole
- Next row: P5, K to last 5 sts, P5.
- Next row: P to end.
- Repeat these 2 rows until the armhole section measures 14″ (35.6cm).

LEFT SIDE FRONT
- Work in St st patt for 13″ (33cm), ending with (WS).
- Next row: K2tog, K to end.
- Next row: P across.
- Repeat last 2 rows.
- BO all sts.

RIGHT SIDE BACK
- With US 9 needles and A, CO 24 (26, 28, 30, 32) sts.
- Work in St st patt for 14″ (35.6cm), ending with (WS).

Armhole
- Next row: P5, K to last 5 sts, P5.
- Next row: P to end.
- Repeat these 2 rows until the armhole section measures 14″ (35.6cm).

RIGHT SIDE FRONT
- Work in St st patt for 13″ (33cm), ending with (WS).
- Next row: K to last 2 sts, K2tog.
- Next row: P across.
- Repeat last 2 rows.
- BO all sts.

SIDE RECTANGLE (MAKE 2)
- With US 8 needles and B, CO 30 sts.
- *K2, P2*, repeat from * to * to end.
- Work in Double Rib patt until work measures 13″ (33cm).
- BO all sts.

FINISHING

If needed, block all pieces to the required sizes. Sew a 14″ (35.5cm) back seam. Fold in half and attach the side rectangles to form the underarm sections (see page 58).

To make an inside facing for the zipper, cast on 4 stitches and work in St st patt for the length of the zipper. Bind off. Pin the facing on the wrong side along front and waist opening. Stitch to secure. Repeat for the other side of the zipper. Alternatively, (WS) pick up sts ½″ from edges and knit 2 rows in St st. BO.

With right side facing, insert zipper between the top layer and facing. Pin and sew through all layers with regular sewing thread.

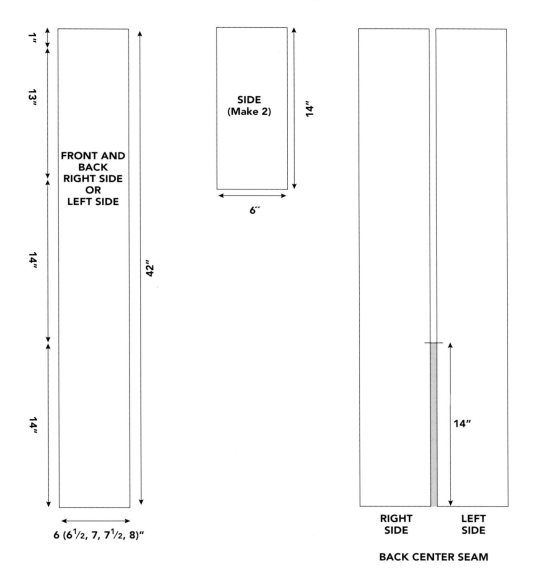

1"

13"

FRONT AND
BACK
RIGHT SIDE
OR
LEFT SIDE

14"

42"

14"

6 (6½, 7, 7½, 8)"

SIDE
(Make 2)

14"

6″

RIGHT
SIDE

LEFT
SIDE

14"

BACK CENTER SEAM

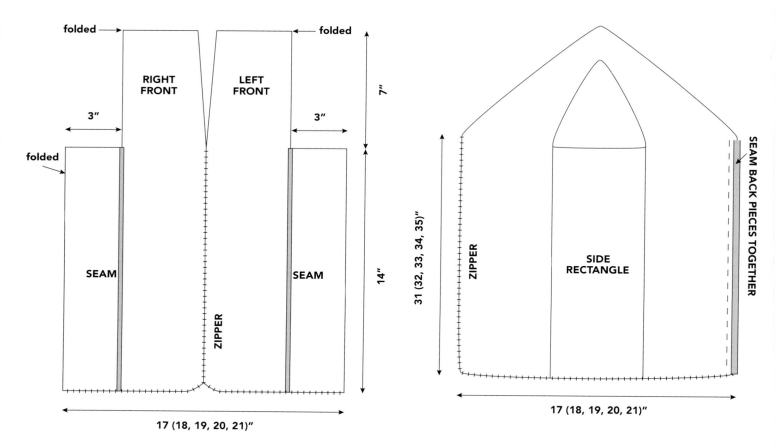

folded → ← folded

RIGHT FRONT **LEFT FRONT**

3" 3"

folded

SEAM **SEAM**

ZIPPER

7"

14"

17 (18, 19, 20, 21)"

ZIPPER

SIDE RECTANGLE

31 (32, 33, 34, 35)"

SEAM BACK PIECES TOGETHER

17 (18, 19, 20, 21)"

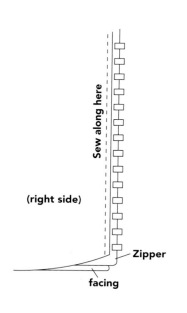

Sew along here

(right side)

Zipper

facing

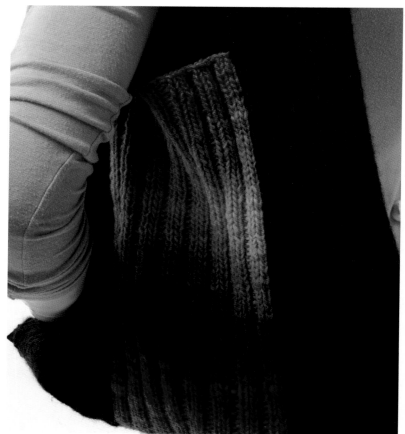

scarves

THE NEXT TIME YOU KNIT A SCARF, WOULD YOU LIKE TO try a different style? Here are three new designs for your next scarf-making experience. Each uniquely designed scarf is knit with a different technique and style.

The Fancy Border Scarf is created with an openwork lace pattern. The yarn is hand-sewn around the edges for the unique border. The Ruffled Neck Scarf incorporates keyhole openings and layers of ruffles for a dressy scarf style and fashionable wear. For a mod look, try the Drawstring Balls Scarf. This one-of-a-kind scarf is knit with colorful yarns in a Seed stitch pattern. Small drawstring balls are hung with beaded strands from the edges. Each special scarf will enhance your knitting skills and complement your wardrobe.

drawstring balls scarf

THE DRAWSTRING BALLS SCARF draws its inspiration from a colorful quilting project. It's created with an array of vibrant yarns using a Seed stitch pattern. Unique drawstring balls, used to create the fringe, are knit from small rectangles and are wonderful as a border treatment. Materials used in this project come from a needlepoint supply store, where yarns are available in a variety of colors and shades. Mixing and matching colors creates a rich-looking scarf that is guaranteed to brighten any outfit.

drawstring balls scarf

SKILL LEVEL

Easy

FINISHED MEASUREMENTS

- 5˝ (7.5cm) wide × 58˝ (147cm) long

YARN

- 2 skeins each 4 ply Appleton *Tapestry Wool* 30yds (27m) / (100% wool) Colors: 253 Grass Green, 562 Sky Blue, 862 Coral, 601 Mauve, and 604 Mauve

YARDAGE

- 60yds (55m) per color

NEEDLES

- One pair size US 6 (4mm) needles, or size to obtain gauge
- Tapestry needle

GAUGE

- 22 sts and 24 rows = 4˝ (10cm) over Seed stitch patt using size US 6 (4mm) needles

FINISHING MATERIALS

- 200 – 250 beads ¹⁄₁₀˝

- Small amount of fiberfill
- Sewing needle and thread

SEED STITCH PATTERN

- Row 1: *K1, P1* rep from * to * to end.
- Row 2: K the P sts and P the K sts.
- Repeat rows 1 & 2.

STOCKINETTE STITCH PATTERN

- Row 1: K across.
- Row 2: P across.
- Repeat Rows 1 and 2.

drawstring balls scarf pattern

SCARF

- With US 6 needles, CO 28 sts.
- Row 1: *K1, P1*, repeat from * to * to end.
- Row 2: *P1, K1*, repeat from * to * to end.
- Repeat Rows 1 and 2, changing yarn randomly, until piece measures 58˝ (147cm).
- BO all sts.

DRAWSTRING BALLS

- CO (see Loop Cast On, page 84) 14 sts.
- Work in St st patt for 5 rows.
- With tapestry needle, thread yarn through rem sts and pull tightly to secure. Repeat with cast-on loops.
- Stuff the ball with cotton or fiberfill.

- Stitch side edges tog.
- Create 18 drawstring balls in different color yarns.

FINISHING

With mauve 604, blanket stitch or crab stitch (page 89) along the scarf border. Sew a beaded string to each ball with regular sewing needle and thread. Sew beaded strings evenly along the scarf edges.

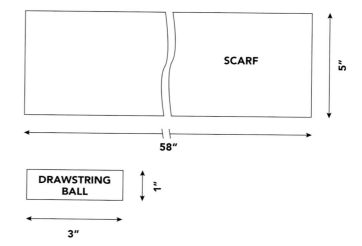

fancy border scarf

TODAY'S KNITTERS ARE BLESSED WITH A VARIETY OF beautiful yarns. Bouclerone, a uniquely decorative yarn, is used to make the border of this project. This wool blend yarn works well as basic trim or fancy fringe. The Merino Frappe yarn is ideal for knitters who want experience with knitting a lace pattern. This Fancy Border Scarf blends beautiful yarns in a simple pattern design. Your patience will be rewarded when you complete this gorgeous scarf.

SKILL LEVEL

Easy

FINISHED MEASUREMENTS

- 5" (12.5cm) wide × 70" (178cm) long

YARN

- 1 ball Crystal Palace *Merino Frappe* 140yds (127m) / 50g (80% merino wool, 20% polyamide) Color: 29 (A)

- 1 ball Austermann *Bouclerone* 16.5yds (15m) / 50g (60% virgin wool, 34% acrylic, 6% polyester) Color:105 (B)

YARDAGE

- Crystal Palace: 140yds (127m)
- Austermann: 5yds (4.5m)

NEEDLES

- One pair size US 9 (5.5mm) needles, or size to obtain gauge

GAUGE

- 16 sts and 20 rows = 4" (10cm) with A over Lace stitch patt using size US 9 (5.5mm) needles

LACE STITCH PATTERN

- Row 1: P across.
- Row 2: K1, *K2tog, YO*, repeat from * to *, end K1.
- Repeat Rows 1 and 2.

fancy border scarf pattern

SCARF

- With US 9 needles and A, CO 20 sts.
- Row 1: P across.
- Row 2: K1, *K2tog, YO*, repeat from * to * until last st, end K1.
- Row 3: P to end.
- Repeat Rows 2–3 until scarf measures 70" (178cm), or desired length.
- BO all sts.

FINISHING

Stitch B yarn to the border with matching thread.

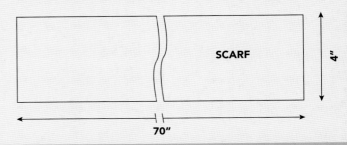

SCARF

70"

4"

ruffled neck scarf

THE RUFFLED NECK SCARF is knit with two different yarns using the same pattern. The red scarf is knit in bulky wool, while the lavender scarf uses a light mohair and wool yarn. The body is knit in a Garter stitch pattern, which incorporates two keyhole openings. The borders are knit with ruffle layers. This versatile scarf can be worn with or without a brooch.

ruffled neck scarf

SKILL LEVEL

Easy

FINISHED MEASUREMENTS

- Red scarf: 6″ (15.25cm) wide × 31″ (78.75cm) long

- Lavender scarf: 5″ (12.75cm) wide × 31″ (78.75cm) long

YARN

- Red scarf: 1 ball *Manos del Uruguay Wool* 135yds (125m) / 100g (100% wool) Color: 054 Burgundy

- Lavender scarf: 1 ball Rowan *Kid Classic* 153yds (140m) / 50g (70% lamb's wool, 26% kid mohair, 4% nylon) Color: 841 Lavender Ice

YARDAGE

- Manos del Uruguay: 135yds (125m)

- Rowan: 150yds (140m)

NEEDLES

- One pair size US 9 (5.5mm) and US 11 (8mm) needles, or size to obtain gauge

GAUGE

- Red Scarf: 14 sts and 20 rows = 4″ (10cm) with *Wool* over Garter stitch patt using size US 9 (5.5mm) needles.

- Lavender Scarf: 18 sts and 28 rows = 4″ (10cm) with *Kid Classic* over Garter stitch patt using size US 9 (5.5mm) needles

STOCKINETTE STITCH PATTERN

- Row 1: K across.

- Row 2: P across.

- Repeat Rows 1 and 2.

GARTER STITCH PATTERN

- K every row.

ruffled neck scarf pattern

SCARF

- With US 11 needles, CO 44 sts.

- Work in St st patt for 4 rows.

- Change to US 9 needles.

- Decrease row: *K2tog, rep from * to end. 22 sts.

- Next row: P1 row and slide all sts onto a holder.

- With US 11 needles, CO 44 sts.

- Work in St st patt for 6 rows.

- Change to US 9 needles.

- Decrease row: *K2tog, rep from * to end. 22 sts.

- Next row: P1 row.

- Join 2 layers: Place holder with sts on top of work, *knit 1 st from holder and 1 st from left needle tog*, repeat from * to * to end. 22 sts.

- Work in Garter st patt until work measures 24˝ (61cm).

Openings

- K7 sts, turn work to the other side, cont working these 7 sts in Garter st patt for 3˝ (7.5cm).

- Rejoin yarn, K next 8 sts, turn work to the other side, cont in Garter st patt for 3˝ (7.5cm).

- Rejoin yarn, K next 7 sts, turn work to the other side, cont in Garter st patt for 3˝ (7.5cm).

- Combine all 22 sts on left needle, K to end.

- Cont in Garter st patt until work measures 29˝ (73.5cm), ending with (WS).

- Change to US 11 needles.

- Increase row: Inc 1 st on every st. 44 sts.

- Work 3 more rows in St st patt.

- BO all sts loosely.

- With (WS) facing, pick up 22 sts right before the inc row.

- Next row: P1 row.

- Increase row: Inc 1 st on every st. 44 sts.

- Work 5 more rows in St st patt.

- BO all sts loosely.

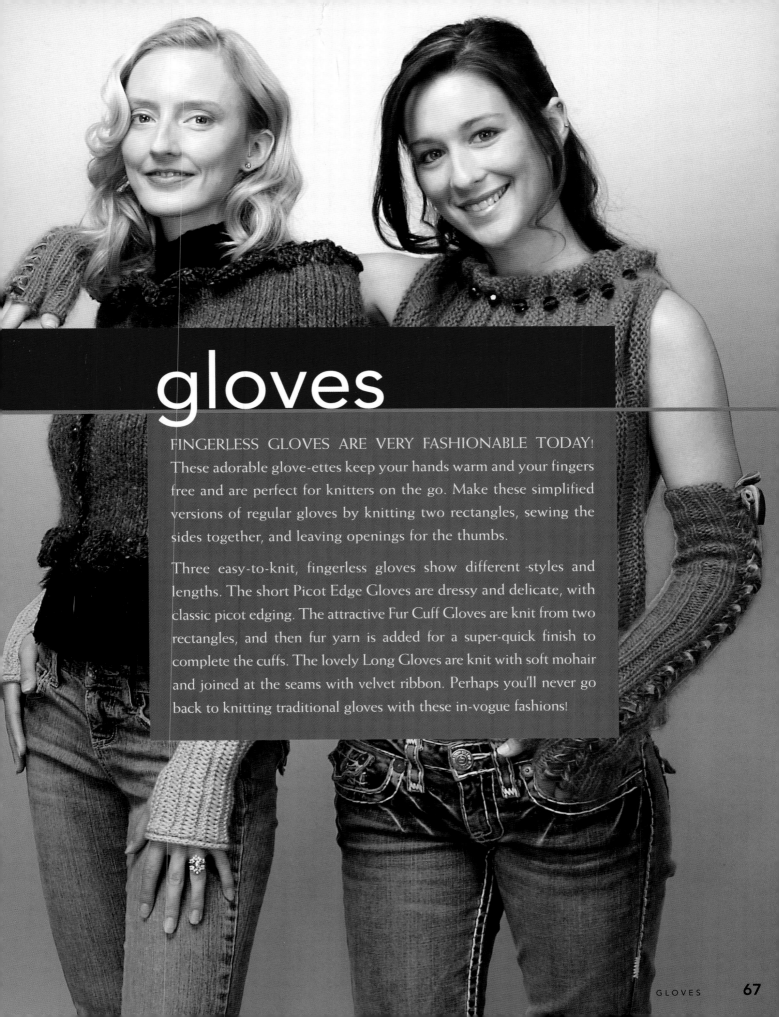

gloves

FINGERLESS GLOVES ARE VERY FASHIONABLE TODAY! These adorable glove-ettes keep your hands warm and your fingers free and are perfect for knitters on the go. Make these simplified versions of regular gloves by knitting two rectangles, sewing the sides together, and leaving openings for the thumbs.

Three easy-to-knit, fingerless gloves show different styles and lengths. The short Picot Edge Gloves are dressy and delicate, with classic picot edging. The attractive Fur Cuff Gloves are knit from two rectangles, and then fur yarn is added for a super-quick finish to complete the cuffs. The lovely Long Gloves are knit with soft mohair and joined at the seams with velvet ribbon. Perhaps you'll never go back to knitting traditional gloves with these in-vogue fashions!

fur cuff gloves

HERE'S A UNIQUE WAY TO KNIT fingerless gloves. Instead of working in rounds, the gloves are created by knitting two matching rectangles sideways. A unique stitch pattern, similar to the elasticity of ribbing, allows for a stretchable fit. Soft merino wool gives these gloves a dressy look and feel. The finish is quick and easy—simply sew the side seams and attach furry cuffs, if desired. These fancy Fur Cuff Gloves are a fashion must!

A reverse view without furry cuffs.

fur cuff gloves

SKILL LEVEL

Beginner

SIZES

S (M, L, XL)

FINISHED MEASUREMENTS

- 8˝ (20cm) long

- 6 (7, 8, 9)˝ / 15 (17.5, 20, 23)cm around palms

YARN

- 1 ball Jaeger *Matchmaker* 131yds (120m) / 50g (100% merino wool) Color: 883 (A)

- 1 ball Plymouth *Foxy* 17yds (15m) / 40g (100% acrylic) Color: 6 (B)

YARDAGE

- Jaeger: 100yds (92m)

- Plymouth: 3yds (2.75m)

NEEDLES

- One pair size US 5 (3.75mm) and US 15 (10mm) needles, or size to obtain gauge

GAUGE

- 24 sts and 30 rows = 4˝ (10cm) with A over Stockinette stitch patt using size US 5 (3.75mm) needles

- 8 sts and 8 rows = 4˝ (10cm) with B over Stockinette stitch patt using size US 15 (10mm) needles

STOCKINETTE STITCH PATTERN

- Row 1: K across.

- Row 2: P across.

- Repeat Rows 1 and 2.

fur cuff gloves pattern

FRONT AND BACK (MAKE 2)

- With US 5 needles and A, CO 45 sts.

- Row 1: P5, K35, P5.

- Row 2: K5, P35, K5.

- Row 3: P5, K35, P5.

- Row 4: K to end.

- Row 5: P5, Drop st (page 87) to last 5, P5.

- Row 6: K to end.

- Repeat last 6 rows 7 (8, 9, 10) times.

- BO all sts.

FUR CUFF (MAKE 2)

- With US 15 needles and B, CO 2 sts.

- K every row until length matches glove width.

- BO all sts.

FINISHING

Stitch side seams together, leaving a 1˝ (2.5cm) hole for the thumb. Sew B to the cuff edges with matching thread.

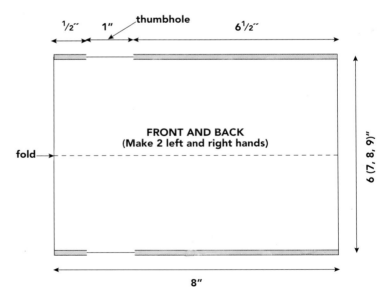

½˝ 1˝ thumbhole 6½˝

FRONT AND BACK
(Make 2 left and right hands)

fold

6 (7, 8, 9)˝

8˝

long gloves

LONG FINGERLESS GLOVES are an ideal fashion accessory with ponchos or sleeveless tops. These fun Long Gloves are easily knit in different lengths for flexible sizing. The glove is knit in soft mohair, worked in Double Ribbing, from identical rectangles. Split openings are knit into the piece, creating a separate room for the thumb. Finish the gloves by weaving a long velvet ribbon along the seams. These gloves are a lovely embellishment for a perfect fashion fit.

long gloves

SKILL LEVEL

Easy

SIZES

S (M, L, XL)

FINISHED MEASUREMENTS

- 21″ (53cm) long

- 6 (7, 8, 9)″ / 15 (17.5, 20, 23)cm around palms

YARN

- 2 (3, 3, 3) balls Artfibers *Basque* 110yds (100m) / 50g (58% silk, 42% super kid mohair) Color: 9

YARDAGE

- 220 (248, 280, 304)yds / 203 (229, 258, 280)m

NEEDLES

- One pair size US 8 (5mm) needles, or size to obtain gauge

GAUGE

- 25 sts and 22 rows = 4″ (10cm) over Ribbing stitch patt using size US 8 (5mm) needles

FINISHING MATERIALS

- 7 yds (6.5m) velvet ribbon ½″ (1.25cm) wide

DOUBLE RIBBING STITCH PATTERN

- Row 1: *K2, P2.

- Repeat from * to end of row.

long gloves pattern

FRONT AND BACK (MAKE 2)

- With US 8 needles, CO 38 (42, 48, 52) sts.

- Row 1: *K2, P2*, repeat from * to *, end K2.

- Row 2: *P2, K2*, repeat from * to *, end P2.

- Repeat Rows 1 and 2 until work measures 20″ (51cm).

Thumb

- Work first 22 (24, 26, 28) sts in Double Rib patt, turn work to other side, cont patt for 1″ (2.5cm), BO.

- Rejoin yarn, work next 10 (10, 12, 12) sts in Double Rib patt, turn work to other side, cont patt for 1″ (2.5cm), BO.

- Rejoin yarn, work remaining 6 (8,10,12) sts in Double Rib patt for 1″ (2.5cm), BO.

FINISHING

Fold the rectangle to match split openings between thumb and palm. Stitch to make separate room for the thumb. Lace ribbon through the length of the glove along the long edges. Stitch pattern is reversible. Turn work to the reverse side before sewing the other glove.

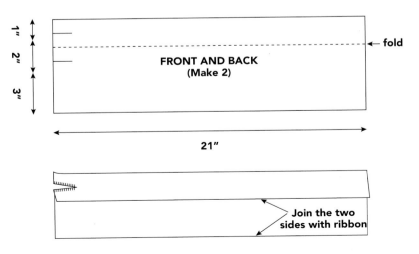

1″ 2″ 3″

FRONT AND BACK (Make 2) ← fold

21″

Join the two sides with ribbon

picot edge glove

WHO SAYS GLOVES HAVE TO BE IDENTICAL TO BE A PAIR? Like twins, there are identical and fraternal gloves. Create these nonidentical, yet perfectly matched, Picot Edge Gloves by alternating the yarn color in the edging and body of the glove. A combination of Ribbing and Picot stitch patterns complement the design. Knit from fine fingering wool yarn, the delicate picot edging adds a classic touch to an easy pattern.

SKILL LEVEL

Easy

SIZES

S (M, L, XL)

MEASUREMENTS

- 6″ (15cm) long
- 6 (7, 8, 9)″ / 15 (17.5, 20, 23)cm around palms

YARN

- 1 ball Rowan *Harris 4 Ply* 120yds (110m) / 25g (100% pure new wool) Color: 2 (A)

- 1 ball Rowan *Harris 4 Ply* 120yds (110m) / 25g (100% pure new wool) Color: 6 (B)

YARDAGE

- 60yds (55m) of each color

NEEDLES

- One pair size US 3 (3.25mm) needles, or size to obtain gauge

GAUGE

- 28 sts and 40 rows = 4″ (10cm) over Stockinette stitch patt using size US 3 (3.25mm) needles

STOCKINETTE STITCH PATTERN

- Row 1: K across.
- Row 2: P across.
- Repeat Rows 1 and 2.

SINGLE RIBBING PATTERN

- Row 1: *P1, K1.
- Repeat from * to end of row.

picot edge gloves pattern

FRONT/BACK (MAKE 2; REVERSE A AND B FOR SECOND GLOVE)

- With A and US 3 needles, CO 60 (70, 80, 90) sts.
- Row 1: K across.
- Row 2: P across.

Picot Edge

- Row 3: K1, *K2tog, YO*, repeat from * to *, K1.
- Row 4: P across.

- Row 5: K across.
- Row 6: P across.

FRONT/BACK CONTINUED

Change to B and cont in Single Rib patt until work measures 6″ (15cm), ending with (WS).

K4 rows. BO all sts.

FINISHING

Stitch side seams together, leaving a 1″ (2.5cm) hole for the thumb. For Picot Edge, turn under 0.5″ (1.25cm) hem and stitch to secure.

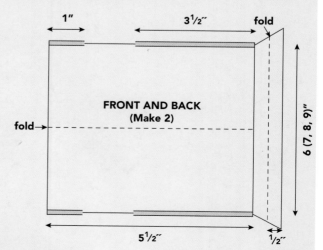

FRONT AND BACK
(Make 2)

1″ 3½″ fold

fold

6 (7, 8, 9)″

5½″ ½″

bags

HERE ARE TWO GOOD REASONS FOR KNITTING A BAG: it's a good opportunity to try out complicated stitch patterns, and because only a small amount of yarn is required, you can use a more luxurious yarn than what you would normally use for knitting a sweater. This chapter teaches you three simple ways to construct a bag from one or more knitted rectangles, which can be used as a starting point for many variations.

Begin with the easy Check Pattern Bag, which is knit from two rectangles using alternating knit and purl stitches. The useful Drawstring Bag is knit in a Stockinette stitch pattern with a lace opening for the drawstring. When you're ready to try cable knitting, make the Cable Pattern Bag with two different color yarns. These fashionable handbags are quick and rewarding to make and are something that you'll treasure forever!

KNIT TRICKS!

cable pattern bag

THE CABLE PATTERN BAG uses a handbag formula that always works: knit a rectangle with a sturdy, darker color yarn for the base, then knit two more rectangles with a contrasting yarn for the bag body. The practical pattern can be applied to different cable designs. It's easy to make the bag larger by knitting the rectangle sides longer. Fold the knit fabric through the slotted handles and sew for a super-quick assembly. Stylish for any occasion, this handbag is versatile and indispensable.

cable pattern bag

SKILL LEVEL

Advanced Beginner

FINISHED MEASUREMENTS

- 12″ (30.5cm) base × 9″ (23cm) high

YARN

- 1 ball Fiber Company *Terra* 100yds (91m) / 50g (60% merino, 20% baby alpaca, 20% silk) Color: Black Walnut (A)

- 2 skeins Appleton *Tapestry Wool* 30yds (27m) / 4ply (100% wool) Color: 561 Sky Blue (B)

YARDAGE

- Fiber Company: 100yds (91m)

- Appleton: 60yds (55m)

NEEDLES

- One pair size US 9 (5.5mm) and US 6 (4mm) needles, or size to obtain gauge

- Cable needle

GAUGE

- 28 sts and 22 rows = 4″ (10cm) with A over Cable stitch patt using size US 9 (5.5mm) needles

- 30 sts and 24 rows = 4″ (10cm) with B over Cable stitch patt using US 6 (4mm) needles

FINISHING MATERIALS

- 1 pair wooden slotted handles 12″ (30.5cm) × 4″ (10cm)

cable pattern bag pattern

BOTTOM

- With A and US 9 needles, CO 48 sts.

- Rows 1 and 3: P2, *K8, P4*, repeat from * to * until last 10 sts, K8, P2.

- Rows 2 and 4: K2, *P8, K4*, repeat from * to * until last 10 sts, P8, K2.

- Row 5: P2 *slide 4 sts onto cable needle, place in front, K4, K4 from cable needle, P4*, repeat from * to *, P2.

- Rows 6, 8, and 10: Rep Row 2.

- Rows 7 and 9: Rep Row 1.

- Repeat last 10 rows until work measures 12″ (30.5cm).

- BO all sts.

SIDE (MAKE 2)

- With B and US 6 needles, CO 90 sts.

- Rows 1 and 3: P2, *K6, P4*, repeat from * to * until last 8 sts, K6, P2.

- Rows 2 and 4: K2, *P6, K4*, repeat from * to * until last 8 sts, P6, K2.

- Row 5: P2, *slide 3 sts onto cable needle, place in front, K3, K3 from cable needle, P4*, repeat from * to *, P2.

- Rows 6, 8, and 10: Rep Row 2.

- Rows 7 and 9: Rep Row 1.

- Repeat last 10 rows until work measures 7″ (17.75cm).

- BO all sts.

FINISHING

With (WS) facing, fold bottom in half. Sew side edges of bottom to the cast-on edges of the sides. Sew the side seams. Turn the bag over to (RS), slide the top edges into the slotted handle, and fold over 1.5″ (3.8cm). Stitch to secure the handles.

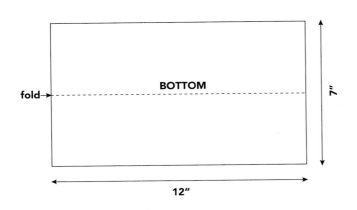

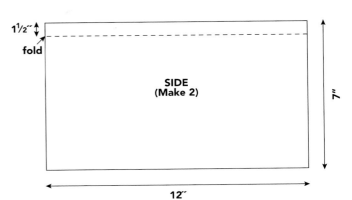

check pattern bag

THE CHECK PATTERN BAG is a gratifying and easy project for first-time knitters. Knit the bag from just one rectangle in a DK weight with large needles. The wool-silk-cashmere blend yarn knits into a beautiful textural fabric by working a series of knit and purl stitches on alternating rows. Finishing is quick, with just two side seams. Sew on handles, and you're on your way!

check pattern bag

SKILL LEVEL

Beginner

FINISHED MEASUREMENTS

- 13″ (33cm) base × 7″ (17.75cm) high

YARN

- 2 balls Jo Sharp *Silkroad DK Tweed* 135yds (147m) / 50g (85% wool, 10% silk, 5% cashmere) Color: 400

YARDAGE

- 246yds (229m)

NEEDLES

- One pair size US 11 (8mm) needles, or size to obtain gauge

GAUGE

- 12 sts and 16 rows = 4″ (10cm) over Check pattern using size US 11 (8mm) needles

FINISHING MATERIALS

- 1 pair handles 6″ (15cm) × 5″ (12.75cm)

STOCKINETTE STITCH PATTERN

- Row 1: K across.
- Row 2: P across.
- Repeat Rows 1 and 2.

check pattern bag pattern

FRONT OR BACK

- With US 11 needles and 3 strands of *Silkroad DK Tweed* held tog, CO 40 sts.
- Work 4 rows in St st patt.

Check Pattern (8 rows)

- Rows 1, 2, 3, 4: *K4, P4*, repeat from * to * to end.
- Rows 5, 6, 7, 8: *P4, K4*, repeat from * to * to end.
- Repeat Check patt 6 more times.
- Work 4 rows in St st patt.
- BO all sts.

FINISHING

With (WS) facing, sew side seams tog on an angle, so seam allowance grows from ½″ (1.24cm) at the bottom to 1½″ (3.75cm) at the top. Turn bag over to the (RS) and stitch to secure handles. (Optional: stitch on small tags to secure handles. Use fabric, felt, or knitted panels. To knit, CO 5 stitches single strand and BO when tag measures 1½″.)

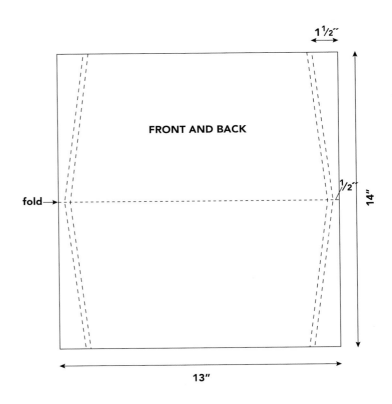

1½″

FRONT AND BACK

fold →

½″

14″

13″

drawstring bag

THIS EASY DRAWSTRING BAG is constructed from two rectangles. The large rectangle forms the body, and the long thin piece is knit for the strap/side gusset. Rich bouclé yarn is worked in Stockinette stitch, creating a thick knit fabric for everyday use. Lace rows create the openings for weaving the color-contrasting drawstring cord. Assembly is as easy as sewing the sides to the gusset strap. Stylish yet durable, this purse makes a great carryall for all your essentials.

SKILL LEVEL

Easy

FINISHED MEASUREMENTS

- 14″ (35.6cm) wide × 8″ (20cm) high × 3″ (7.5cm) deep

YARN

- 1 ball Lion Brand *Color Waves* 125yds (118m) / 85g (83% acrylic, 17% polyester) Color: 350 Night Sky (A)

- 1 ball Malabrigo *Red Mahogany* 216yds (196m) / 3.5oz (100% merino wool) Color: Red Mahogany (B)

YARDAGE

- Lion Brand: 125yds (118m)
- Malabrigo: 4yds (3.5m)

NEEDLES

- One pair size US 10 (6mm) needles and US 9 (5.5mm) double-pointed needles, or size to obtain gauge

GAUGE

- 12 sts and 16 rows = 4″ (10cm) with A over Stockinette stitch patt using size US 10 (6mm) needles

- 18 sts and 23 rows = 4″ (10cm) with B over Stockinette stitch patt using size US 9 (5.5mm) needles

STOCKINETTE STITCH PATTERN

- Row 1: K across.
- Row 2: P across.
- Repeat Rows 1 and 2.

drawstring bag pattern

FRONT/BACK

- With US 10 needles and A, CO 42 sts.

- Rows 1–6: Work in St st patt.

Lace Row

- Row 11: Work Drop st (page 87) across.

- Row 12: P across.

FRONT/BACK CONTINUED

- Cont in St st patt until work measures 17½″ (44cm), ending with (WS).

- Next row: Work Drop st across.

- Work next 5 rows in St st patt.

- BO all sts.

SHOULDER STRAP

- With US 10 needles and A, CO 12 sts.

- Cont in St st patt until work measures 36″ (91cm). (For longer strap, adjust length as desired.)

- BO all sts.

DRAWSTRING I-CORD

- With US 9 double-pointed needles and B, CO 3 sts.

- Work in I-cord (page 90) until string measures 32″ (81cm) long.

- BO. Tie knots at ends.

FINISHING

With (WS) facing, stitch side seams and shoulder strap tog. From the (RS), thread the drawstring through the openings of the lace row and tie in a bow.

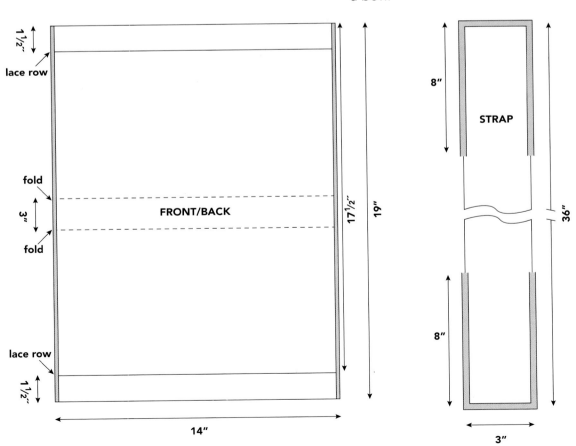

knitting basics

THIS CHAPTER TEACHES FIRST-TIME KNITTERS HOW to knit and provides a refresher for beginner knitters. In this chapter are many of the required knitting techniques for the book's 25 projects. Step-by-step color photographs show you each technique. Reverse right-hand instructions for left-hand knitters.

The basics include the slipknot, two cast-on methods, binding off, and knit and purl stitches. Elementary shaping in this book utilizes yarn over increasing and knit-two-together decreasing. Progress to fundamental techniques with drop stitches, button-holes, and cables. Learn decorative methods through crochet chain, single crochet, crab stitch, and I-cord skills. Finalize your knitting basics with horizontal invisible seams and blocking. With practice, you will enjoy knitting and be able to create chic knitwear from simple rectangles.

Slipknot

Begin knitting by making a basic slipknot. Fasten the knot securely on the needle but loose enough to allow the stitches to slide easily.

1. To make a slipknot, wrap the yarn around your index and middle fingers 2 times.

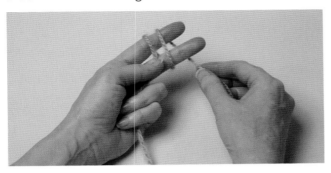

2. Pull the yarn attached to the ball through the loop.

3. Place the needle in the loop and tighten the knot on the needle. Pull the knot snug, but not too tight. The slipknot is the first cast-on stitch.

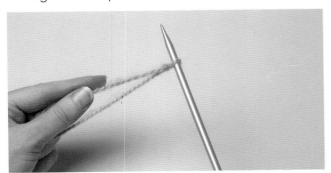

Long-Tail Cast On

To begin knitting, you need to cast on the required number of stitches called for in the pattern. The long-tail cast on uses a tail and the strand attached to the ball to place stitches on the needle. The knitting symbol for cast on is CO.

1. Wrap the tail end clockwise around your left thumb and the ball yarn counterclockwise around your index finger to form a slingshot. Hold both strands securely in the palm of your left hand.

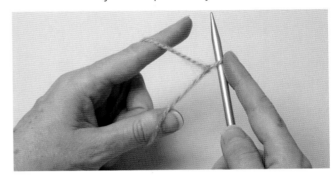

2. Insert the tip of the needle under the yarn on your thumb and lift.

3. Hook the tip of the needle behind the yarn on your index finger from top to bottom and pull the needle back through the loop on your thumb. Slip the loop off your thumb and gently tighten the stitch on the needle.

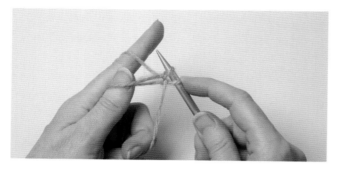

4. Repeat Steps 1–3 until the required number of stitches is cast on the needle.

Loop Cast On

There are many techniques for casting on stitches. The backward loop is a variation for casting on in the middle of a row. This technique is one of the steps used in creating a buttonhole.

1. Loop the yarn attached to the ball clockwise around your left thumb.

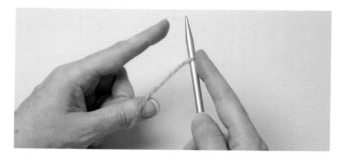

2. Slip the needle tip under the loop of yarn around your left thumb.

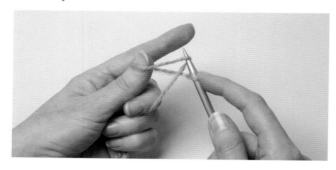

3. Lift the yarn off your thumb and pull gently to make a new cast-on stitch.

Binding Off

Binding off prevents a knitted garment from unraveling, secures the stitches on your knitwear, and leaves a clean, decorative edge. The knitting symbol for binding off is BO.

1. Work the next 2 stitches.

2. Insert the tip of the left-hand needle into the first stitch. Then lift the stitch over the second stitch and off the right-hand needle.

3. Repeat Steps 1 and 2 until 1 stitch remains. Lift the last stitch off the needle and cut the yarn, leaving a 6″ (15cm) tail. Thread the yarn through the last stitch and make a knot. Weave in the remaining tail.

Knit Stitch

The knit stitch is one of two basic knitting stitches. When making a knit stitch, always keep the yarn behind the needles. The knitting symbol for the knit stitch is K.

1. Insert the right-hand needle from left to right (knitwise) into the first cast-on stitch.

2. Always keep the yarn behind the needles for a knit stitch. Wrap the yarn counterclockwise around the tip of the right-hand needle and gently pull the yarn down between the 2 needles.

3. Insert the tip of the right-hand needle up through the center of the cast-on stitch and lift the stitch off the left-hand needle. Repeat Steps 1–3 until all the knit stitches are on the right-hand needle.

Purl Stitch

The purl stitch is the second basic stitch in knitting. When purling, keep the yarn in front of the needles. The knitting symbol for the purl stitch is P.

1. With the yarn in front and the needle with the stitches in your left hand, insert the right-hand needle (purlwise) through the first stitch from right to left.

2. Wrap the yarn counterclockwise around the tip of the right-hand needle.

3. Draw the tip of the right-hand needle back through the stitch and slide the stitch off the left-hand needle. Repeat Steps 1–3 until all the purl stitches are on the right-hand needle.

Yarn Over Increase

A yarn over increase is an easy way to create an increase or eyelet between two knit stitches. It is also used for lacy patterns, buttonholes, or decorative purposes. The knitting symbol for yarn over is YO.

1. Bring the yarn forward between the 2 needles, as if to purl.

2. Wrap the yarn counterclockwise around the right-hand needle from front to back.

3. Knit the next stitch as usual and complete the row. You have created a hole between 2 knit stitches, thus completing a yarn over increase.

Decreasing

Knitting two stitches together will produce a stitch that slants to the right and reduces the number of stitches by one. The knitting symbol for this decreasing technique is K2tog.

1. Insert the right-hand needle from left to right (knitwise) through 2 stitches together.

2. Wrap the yarn counterclockwise around the tip of the right-hand needle.

3. Knit as usual and lift the original 2 stitches off the left-hand needle. The stitches are decreased to 1 stitch on the right-hand needle. The result is a decrease that slants to the right.

Drop Stitch

The drop stitch technique is used to create a pattern of open vertical stripes in a garment, producing a lace effect.

1. Insert right needle knitwise into the stitch.

2. Wrap the yarn counterclockwise around the right needle twice. Slip the wrapped loops off the left needle and continue across the row. (For the next row, pull the wrapped loops to the full extent while knitting.)

Buttonholes

Create a small buttonhole by binding off two or more stitches and then casting on the same number of stitches to replace them.

1. Work to the position of the buttonhole.

2. Bind off the number of stitches required and continue to the end of the row.

3. Work to the position of the bound-off stitches and turn the work. Use the loop cast on method to recast on the same number of stitches that were bound off in Step 2. Bring the yarn forward. Turn the work again so that the cast-on stitches are on the right needle. Continue working across the row.

Chain Stitch

The chain stitch in crochet is similar to the cast-on stitch in knitting. This stitch is the basis for the foundation chain. The symbol in crochet for the chain stitch is CH.

1. Make a slipknot, slide the hook through the loop, and hook the yarn.

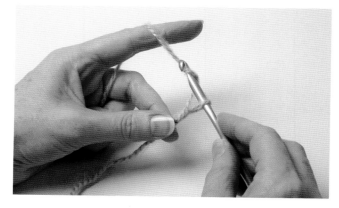

2. Draw the hook and yarn through the loop to begin the chain.

3. Repeat Step 2 by drawing the yarn on the hook through all the chains on the row.

Single Crochet

The single crochet stitch is one of the most basic stitches in crochet. This fundamental stitch creates a firm, tight fabric that is ideal for projects requiring close stitching. The symbol in crochet for the single crochet stitch is SC.

1. Skip the last chain made and insert the hook into the next chain.

2. Hook the yarn and draw a loop through the first stitch.

3. Hook the yarn again and draw through 2 loops. One loop remains on the hook. Continue until you have completed the desired number of stitches called for in the pattern.

Crab Stitch

A crab stitch works a single crochet stitch from left to right, creating a sturdy, decorative edge for your knitting.

1. Insert the hook into the next stitch to be crocheted from front to back. You have 2 loops on the hook.

2. Yarn over and draw the hook through 2 loops.

3. Repeat steps 1 and 2 until the edge is complete. The result is a clean, decorative edge suitable for tops and pullovers.

I-Cord

An I-cord is a narrow knitted tube or cord that is made with two double-pointed needles. It's usually used to make purse handles, shoulder straps, and drawstrings.

1. Cast on 3 stitches onto double-pointed needles.

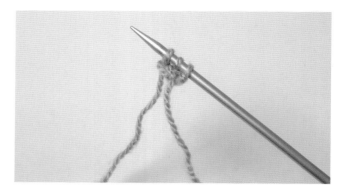

2. Knit the 3 stitches but do not turn.

3. Slide the stitches back to the other pointed end of the needle and knit the row again. Pull the first knit stitch tight for every row. Work until the cord is the desired length.

Blocking

Blocking your knitwear is important, as it will prevent curling and shrinking of your knitted garment. Place your garment (wrong side up) on a board or towel. Insert rustproof pins to block to the desired shape and size. Spray or steam your garment with water, pat dry, and cover. When the garment is completely dry, blocking is complete.

Cables

A cable stitch creates interesting stitch patterns in your knitted garment. This example demonstrates an eight-stitch cable worked with two groups of four stitches. Cables are worked with a cable needle.

1. Work to the desired cable position (right side). With the cable needle in front, insert it (purlwise) into the next group of 4 stitches and slip them off the left needle.

2. Keep the cable in front as you knit the next group of 4 stitches.

3. Knit the group of 4 stitches on the cable needle.

4. Repeat steps 1-3 to create a cable that twists to the left.

Horizontal Invisible Seam

The invisible seam is a simple way to join knitted pieces. It results in a flexible, nearly undetectable seam. This stitch requires both pieces to have the same number of rows.

1. Place the knitted pieces side by side (right side facing). Insert the needle from back to front into the corner stitch 2 times to anchor the stitch.

2. Insert the needle under the horizontal bar between the 2 end stitches on the opposite side.

3. Continue inserting the needle on alternate sides where it last emerged and exit 2 rows higher. Pull yarn ends to join side seams together. Weave in any loose ends.

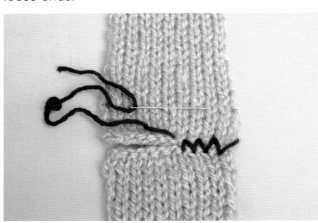

abbreviations

Below is a list of common abbreviations used in this book.
Remember to read each pattern completely before you begin knitting.

* *—repeat instructions between asterisks

approx—approximately

BO—bind off

cm—centimeter(s)

CO—cast on

cont—continue

dec—decrease

g—gram

Garter st—knit or purl every row

"—inch

inc—increase

K—knit

K2tog—knit 2 stitches together

m—meter(s)

mm—millimeter(s)

P—purl

P2tog—Purl 2 stitches together

patt—pattern

pwise—purlwise

rem—remaining

rep—repeat

rep from *—repeat instruction after *

rnd(s)—round(s)

(RS)—right side

sl st—slip stitch

Sl 1—slip 1 stitch knitwise

Sl 1, K1, PSSO or SKP—slip 1 stitch, knit 1 stitch, pass slipped

st(s)—stitch(es)

St st—Stockinette stitch (knit 1 row, purl 1 row; repeat)

tog—together

Tw2L—Twist 2 Left: slip 1 stitch, place in front, knit next stitch from left needle, knit skipped stitch

Tw2R—Twist 2 Right: slip 1 stitch, place in back, knit next stitch from left needle, knit skipped stitch

work even—continue in pattern without increasing or decreasing

(WS)—wrong side

yd(s)—yard(s)

YO—yarn over

resources

For a list of other fine books from C&T Publishing, ask for a free catalog:
C&T Publishing, Inc.
P.O. Box 1456
Lafayette, CA 94549
(800) 284-1114
Email: ctinfo@ctpub.com
Website: www.ctpub.com

C&T Publishing's professional photography services are now available to the public. Visit us at www.ctmediaservices.com

Artfibers
124 Sutter Street
San Francisco, CA 94104
ph 415.956.6319
fx 415.421.1734
free 888.326.1112
www.artfibers.com

Bouton d'Or
distributed by
Anny Blatt USA
7796 Boardwalk
Brighton, MI 48116
ph 248.486.6160
fx 248.486.6165
www.boutondor.com

Cascade Yarns
1224 Andover Park E
Tukwila, WA 98188
www.cascadeyarns.com

Crystal Palace Yarns
160 23rd Street
Richmond, CA 94804
ph 510.237.9988
www.straw.com

Filatura Di Crosa
distributed by Tahki
• Stacy Charles, Inc.
70-30 80th St., Building 36
Ridgewood, NY 11385
ph 800.338.yarn
www.tahkistacycharles.com

JCA Distribution
35 Scales Lane
Townsend, MA 01469-1094
ph 978-597-8794
www.josharp.com.au

Lion Brand Yarns
135 Kero Road
Carlstadt, NJ 07072
ph 800.258.YARN (9276)
www.lionbrand.com

Malabrigo Yarn
ph 786.866.6187
www.malabrigoyarn.com

Manos del Uruguay
www.manos.com.uy

Noro
distributed by Knitting Fever, Inc.
315 Bayview Avenue
Amityville, NY 11701
ph 516.546.3600
fx 516.546.6871
www.knittingfever.com

Rowan Yarns
distributed by Westminster Fibers, Inc.
4 Townsend Avenue, Unit 8
Nashua, NH 03063
ph 800.445.9276
www.knitrowan

Skacel Collection, Inc.
P.O. Box 88110
Seattle, WA 98138
ph 800.255.1278

about the author

Photo by Paul Wat.

Rebecca started knitting and crocheting at the age of five or six. Having lived and received her education in three different continents—Asia, Europe, and North America—she has been exposed to a variety of cultures, as well as various fashion styles and knitting techniques. In addition, she has great passion for the art of origami and quilting, which has tremendous influence on the construction methods and choice of colors of her knits. Her other titles are *Fantastic Fabric Folding—Innovative Quilting Methods* and *A Fresh Twist on Fabric Folding*. Rebecca currently resides in the San Francisco Bay area with her husband and two children.